A BRIEF HISTORY

OF

CHEMUNG COUNTY

NEW YORK

By AUSBURN TOWNER

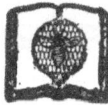

Elmira, New York
Reprinted by New York History Review
2015

A Brief History of Chemung County, New York 1779 -1905 with Index
by Ausburn Towner

Reprinted by New York History Review, originally published in 1907

ISBN: 978-0-9838487-7-6

Printed in the United States of America.

For Joyce

To the Children of Chemung County
of whom I was one,
I dedicate
this little book, with the wish that their lives may be
as bright and sunny as was mine in "the dearest spot
on Earth to me."

Ausburn Towner.

March, 1907.

Reprinted by
New York History Review
Elmira, New York in 2015

INTRODUCTION

Local history is fleeting and evanescent. Events of one day, even considered of supreme importance at the time, are forgotten the next day, and soon drop into oblivion. Any effort to recall them, after years have passed, entails tireless and exhaustive research amongst the files of musty, old newspapers, private memoranda, public records, and, best of all, the interviewing and arousing the recollections of elderly persons; preferably ladies, for their memories are usually very retentive and are seldom found inaccurate. Very much that follows is from the remembrances of old ladies; who knew the country in their girlhood; when it was pretty much all woods and swamps. Interviews with them could only be characterized as delicious. If there could be reproduced only one-half of all they have recalled, it would form a book many times the size of this; and if their names could be given, they would be recognized as belonging to some of the oldest and best-known families of the county.

Seldom does a company assemble socially for a quiet visit that the discussion of "old times" does not come up during the gathering, and those most eagerly listened to are the ones who can tell the most about the periods when our "grandfathers lived." It is a subject not particularly valuable, perhaps with some exceptions, but always interesting and entertaining.

It will be found that children are always attracted toward subjects of this character, and it is safe to place such memories in their keeping. They can then tell all about their homes and the people dwelling thereabouts, and transmit their knowledge to an indefinite posterity. When they are fully informed concerning these matters in their own localities, they will be prepared to enter with enthusiasm upon the study of the stories of the larger affairs of the world.

AUSBURN TOWNER.

PART I

The County and Valley during the closing years of the XVIII Century

---

But many of the fathers, who were ancient men, had seen the first house, when the foundation of this house was laid before their eyes.—Ezra, iii., 12.

His echoing axe the settler swung,
  Amid the sea-like solitude,
And, rushing, thundering down were flung
  The Titans of the wood.—Alfred B. Street.

The Closing Years of the XVIII Century.

Beginning with a battle.—Chemung County; N. Y.;
gets its name, as does the river that flows through
it, from an Indian term meaning "Big Horn."' It
is situated in the southern part of New York State;
on the borders of the State of Pennsylvania about
half way between the eastern and western boundaries of New York; in latitude 42° N., its western
line being on the same meridian as that of Washington; D. C., from which longitude is sometimes
reckoned.

It is about 400 square miles in extent.

The whole section of the country in which the
county lies was very little, if at all, known before
1779. It was introduced to the notice of the
country and the world by a brisk and fierce, although
brief battle, that was fought on the hillside three
miles south of Elmira; on August 29 of the year
named, between the American forces and the Indians and Tories, in which the American forces were

---

[1]Two large tusks or horns, relics of long-past ages, were
found embedded in the banks of the river. It is not known
positively, at present, where these horns are now located, although one is said to be near Oswego, N. Y.

victorious.² It is the most important event in
the history of the county and one of the most
important battles of the Revolutionary War. It
broke entirely the power of the Indians in that
region; who were the allies of the English. It also
opened the country for settlers. General Sullivan
found the fertile region occupied by a number of
comfortable villages and there were great crops of
corn, watermelons; and almost every kind of fruit
just about ready to be gathered. In accordance
with his orders he left it a waste and a wilder-
ness.

Many of the soldiers engaged in the battle returned to the valley and made it their permanent
home. But most of the earlier settlers came from

---

²In this conflict, called "The Battle of Newtown," there
were about 4,000 men engaged, an equal number on each
side. The American troops were under the command of
Major-General John Sullivan, and the Indians under that
of the famous Iroquois half-breed, Joseph Brant and Colonel
John Butler. General Washington himself, who knew well
how to fight Indians, laid the plans of the expedition, warn-
ing General Sullivan especially against being ambushed
or surprised in the night. The object of the expedition
into such an unknown country was to punish the Indians
for numerous atrocities they had committed upon the settlers at Wyoming and many other places, and to destroy
their country which had been used to furnish supplies for
the British army. The natural features of the hillside
formed a most admirable spot for the Indians to lay a trap
for the Americans, and they took full advantage of them.
General Sullivan didn't fall into it. He came around the
hill in their rear and flank and utterly routed them. There
were only twenty-five men killed in the fight; it lasted only
a few hours. Why it is called "The Battle of Newtown"
it would be difficult to determine. There was no Newtown
there when the battle was fought. It should be "The
Battle of Chemung." The title is attractive, indigenous,
sonorous, and descriptive. There are any quantity of
Newtowns all over the country. There is only one Chemung.

the neighborhood of Wilkesbarre; Pa., from Orange
County, N. Y., and from the State of Connecticut.

The earliest settlers.—It was a hard journey to
get to the county. There were no roads, and the
river supplied the only means of communication.
In little boats, which they pushed up the stream
with long poles, the early comers made their tedious
and toilsome way. Or they walked, leading their
horses or oxen, who bore all their earthly possessions.

Within ten years after the battle there were a
number of families scattered all through the borders of the county induced to come thither by the
stories the soldiers had spread abroad of the extreme
fruitfulness of the country. They found it equaling
their expectations, and there are many in the
valley now bearing the names of those who, in the
latter years of the eighteenth century, made it
their new home, leaving records that it is
pleasant to recall.³ As all pioneers, they were a

---

³There are some names of all that came, that for many
reasons, deserve recalling and a continuance in our memories. Major WILLIAM WYNKOOP, a Revolutionary soldier,
who was at the battle of Saratoga, who built the first frame
house in the township of Chemung, and the first grist-mill
there, and kept the first tavern. He died in 1827, aged
seventy-four years. Capt. DANIEL McDOWEL, his descendants
now spell it McDowell, a Scotchman, and a Revolutionary
soldier. He was outrageously tortured by the Indians,
who called him "*Keto*" or the "iron man." He also settled
in Chemung Township. ELIJAH BUCK, who gave his name
to Buckville, though the village afterwards became Chemung.
ABNER WELLS, from whom Wellsburg is named. ISAAC
BALDWIN, who, with his eight sons became a power in the
county, of whom we shall hear more later on. LEBEUS
HAMMOND, who is remembered in the name of "Hammond's
Corners," whose miraculous escape from the Indians, not

rude, rough, even quarrelsome, lot of men. They were having a continual struggle with Nature; and had no objection to a physical argument with fists among themselves. It is a matter of tradition that such amusements as horse-racing on Sundays were not unusual among them. That may be hearsay, but it is a matter of record that at the time of which I write there were more distilleries than there were flouring mills and sawmills together, in the county!

In 1786, Gen. James Clinton, who commanded a brigade in the "Battle of Newtown," one of the family of George Clinton, from whom was named the attractive island that once formed a beauty spot in the valley, and who is only remembered now by the name of a street in Elmira; Gen. John Hathorn and John Cantine, Esq., were appointed

---

told of much now, though it deserves to be, makes one's hair stand on end. JOHN BREESE and ASA GILDERSLEEVE, who came to Horseheads from New Jersey. JOHN SLY, who took up some of the richest lands in Southport near the river bank, and became very wealthy. It is a tradition that he and his wife came into the county, both riding one horse, who also bore all their worldly possessions. NATHANIEL SEELY, JR., and his brothers, who left their name and much else besides to a boisterous creek that flows through Southport into the Chemung River. ANDREW GREGG, an Irishman from Enniskellen, whose son Andrew K., became one of the most distinguished lawyers of the State, and a grandson, Gen. William M. Gregg, who was an efficient officer in the Civil War. Gen. MATTHEW CARPENTER was very conspicuous in the early political and military affairs of the county. He served as county clerk for twenty-seven years. A daughter of his, who married Robert Thompson, published a small volume of poems, which with local pride she called "The Lyre of Tioga." It was the first literary effort put forth in the county. Some one with little learning and no critical ability, observed rudely at the time that the author seemed to be a poor speller! ABNER M. HETFIELD, who made the town of Southport more populous by contributing twelve children to the enumeration. His son, Richard, became a character who will long be remembered

commissioners on the part of the State to survey
the lands in the county and to settle disputes that
had arisen among those located there. The family
of General Hathorn are still conspicuous citizens
of the county.

A famine.—In the autumn of 1789 there was
an unusual occurrence in the valley. A famine
prevailed throughout the county! It was occa-
sioned by a severe frost the preceding spring that
destroyed the crops that were expected to be har-
vested. It created great suffering and for many
years was referred to as an event to be remembered
with something like horror. The people lived on
a certain sort of wild bean, which they boiled, and

---

for his many good, if peculiar habits and ways. The GRIS-
SELS, DAVID and ELIJAH, who were very active in the affairs
in Southport, building grist-mills and sawmills. Their
descendants now spell the name Griswold. Then the five
SMITHS, beginning with TIMOTHY, a large family of influence
and importance. BARNABUS TUTHILL and his son Samuel,
on what is now Maple Avenue, in Elmira. JOHN McHENRY
and JOHN and WILLIAM FITZSIMMONS, near neighbors to the
TUTHILLS. DAVID BECKWITH and Gen. SETH MARVIN,
farther up Seely Creek. JONATHAN S. CONKLING, JAMES,
JONAS, and EBENEZER SAYRE, MORDECAI RICKEY, and
JACOB WESTLAKE, making the way clearer for Horseheads.
And in Big Flats, CHRISTIAN MINIER, DAVID REYNOLDS,
TUNIS DOLSON, CALEB GARDNER, CLARK WINANS, JAMES
McNULTY, and GREEN BENTLEY. PETER SWARTWOOD,
the father of Gen. JACOB SWARTWOOD, JOEL THOMAS, ISAAC
and EMANUEL ENNIS, SAMUEL, CORNELIUS and PETER
WESTBROOK, JOHN, DAVID, and WILLIAM HILL, made the
beginnings in Van Ettenville.

⁴There was considerable unoccupied land at that time,
as their report shows, although a large portion was taken up,
showing how rapidly the settlers came into the county.
They surveyed 207,656 acres. Of these, 28,300 acres were
military locations, 159,186 were disposed of to settlers,
and 20,170 acres were vacant. The settlers paid eighteen
pence an acre, which is about equal to the half dollar of to-
day.

on the most nutritious roots they could dig
from the ground. Relief came when the rye began
to form. Two young men died from eating to
excess of this green rye.

Treaty with the Indians.—An important treaty,
the last one of the kind in the East, and a final one
with the Iroquois or Six Nations, was made with
the Indians at Elmira in 1791. It settled forever
all questions that were in dispute in that region
between the Aborigines and the United States
Government. Timothy Pickering who had occupied many distinguished positions under General
and President Washington, represented the Government and many conspicuous Indian leaders and
chiefs were present.[6]

Col. John Hendy.—Col. John Hendy was easily,
for almost fifty years, the most conspicuous character in the county. He settled near Elmira in
1788, and built a cabin, which, although in somewhat of a dilapidated state, is still standing. He
was a very impressive-looking man, two inches over

[5] He served as Adjutant-General of the Revolutionary army
in the New Jersey campaign, was Quartermaster-General during the war, and was in President Washington's Cabinet,
serving as Postmaster-General, Secretary of War and Secretary of State. He had great influence with the Indians
who called him "Con-ni-sau-ti—the sunny side of a hill."

[6] Among these was the famous Seneca Chief RED JACKET,
who got his English name from his delight in wearing a red
coat given him by an English soldier. He was an exceedingly fine orator. The council began its sessions on July
4 and lasted ten days. There were about 1,400 Indians
present. One who was present, standing in the doorway
of Col. JOHN HENDY's cabin, counted them as they passed
up the valley to the west. Part of the time, the council
was held near Newtown creek, and the rest of the time at
a spot still pointed out on Market Street, just east of Madison Avenue, in Elmira.

six feet in height, and to the last as straight as a ramrod. He wore his hair long, falling over his shoulders; and when it became white was very pleasant to look upon. He had been a Revolutionary soldier. His descendants still live in the county. He was always conspicuous in public gatherings, Independence Days, and any parades or other displays. He died in 1840.[7]

Henry Wisner.—Henry Wisner was an Orange County man who early became interested in Chemung County. He acquired a large tract of land in the eastern and western portions of what is now the city of Elmira, and laid out two villages, one on the banks of Newtown Creek, near the site of an ancient Indian village,[8] and another in the vicinity of what is now Main Street, in Elmira. Through his son Jeffrey, and his grandsons, John W. and William Henry, the county profited greatly. The family name, it would appear, has entirely died out.

---

[7] The first white child born in the county made its appearance in COLONEL HENDY's cabin, although it did not remain there. One autumn evening a traveler came along, leading a horse bearing a pillion, on which was a woman with a child in her arms. The couple asked to be cared for, and their request was readily granted. It speedily appeared that some unusual care was needed. When COLONEL HENDY was apprised of the approaching event, he was a little thrown off his balance, but recovering himself with the exclamation, "God bless my soul!" he made the necessary arrangements, and the event was successfully accomplished. The child was named JOHN HENDY HUNT. In three days the strangers took up their journey toward Niagara Falls, where they were bound, with a cradle added to the pillion.

[8] The name of this Indian village was "Kan-a-we-o-la," or "Head on a pole," although it had another designation "Shin-e-do-wa," or "At the Great Plains."

Col. Matthias Hollenbeck.[9]—As has been said,
many of the earliest settlers of the valley came from
the neighborhood of Wilkesbarre, Pa. To a citizen of that place Elmira is very largely, almost
entirely, indebted for starting the development
of business there. Matthias Hollenback, who was
a colonel and a judge in his own locality, with his
large means and business enterprise and sagacity,
sent up into the valley the pioneers that were to
open up the county. He sent his son-in-law,
Stephen Tuttle, his nephews, Robert, Lyman, and
Miles Covell, and his associates in business, Thomas
Mifflin Perry, Guy Maxwell, and Matthew Mc-
Reynolds, the latter of whom built the first brick
house erected in the county; a little west of Main
and West Water Streets, in Elmira. These men
made the first business beginnings of the county
with the outside world, using the only means of
communication then provided, the river, down
which, by the way of the Susquehanna, they sent
to a market in Baltimore, Md., the produce of the
county, grain, plaster, and lumber.

The land was taken up from the banks of the
river, several miles north, and a settlement was
made in the neighborhood of what is now East
Water and Fox Streets and Madison Avenue,

---

[9]MATTHIAS HOLLENBACK was a Virginian by birth, a Revolutionary officer, and was present at the massacre at Wyoming. He was a great friend of JOHN JACOB ASTOR, and engaged with him in a number of trading adventures. By
the use of his large means in starting the commercial life
of the valley, by his name and influence, which extend even
to this day, although he was never even a resident of Chemung County, he is entitled to the grateful and generous
remembrance of all its citizens.

in Elmira. A little west of that locality a ferry
was established that led over the river to the
fields of Northern Pennsylvania, only eight miles
away.[10]

There were other contemporary interests in
Elmira. The Baldwin lands were just west of
those described, the Wisner interests still farther
west; the William Hoffman property next, and
then the Fitch lands.

Jacob Lowman, in 1792, came to the neighborhood of the village and post-office, half way between Elmira and Wellsburg, that now bears the
family name. He acquired a very large landed
property and left numerous descendants.

Religious organizations.—The first church organization of the county was of the Baptist faith, and
was started, although not fully established, by the
Rev. Roswell Gough, or "Goff" or Parson Goff. He
held meetings and preached in the neighborhood
of his home between Wellsburg and Chemung as
early as 1790. On this same farm was accomplished
the first grinding of wheat in the county. It was
in very primitive style. A stump of a tree was hol-
lowed at the top; and the grain ground after the
manner of the Indians, with heavy clubs. In 1795
the Rev. Daniel Thatcher came in to the county

---

[10]This ferry was kept for many years by a German named
Kline, who also kept a tavern on the corner of Fox Street.
When his services as ferryman were required, and he was
called, his invariable reply was "treckly." It sounded something like "directly," but his slow actions seemed to indicate
some other meaning, and it was used so frequently that it
became all over the country something of a by-word or
slang that could be made to mean anything. Kline afterwards kept a tavern at Horsehead.

under the auspices of the Presbyterian Board of
Missions. This was the first small beginning of
what has grown now into the powerful First Presbyterian Church of Elmira. Mr. Thatcher was followed in a year or two by the Rev. Brinton Paine
who; in other relations of life became a strong factor
in the development of the region.

New geographical divisions.—In that ancient
time all that portion of the State, a rather indis-
tinct and indeterminate quantity, lying west of
the Hudson River and east of the central lake
region, excepting the counties of Albany, Ulster,
and Orange, was called Montgomery County, named
after General Montgomery, the hero of Quebec.
The township of Chemung was created in 1788, in
this county, and comprised almost precisely the
territory of what is now Chemung County, with a
portion of Schuyler County added. Although it
was fifty-three square miles in extent, it contained
less than one thousand inhabitants.

Two years afterward the village of Newtown
was laid out by Henry Wisner. It was the beginning of the present flourishing city of Elmira, and
was not much of an undertaking. There was what
is now called Sullivan Street, named in honor of
the General who fought the battle of Newtown,
and was the central highway toward the lake
region and the road that ran beside the river toward
the west, with two or three other lanes, nameless
then and nameless now.

A portion of Montgomery County was taken by
act of February 16, 1791, to form a new county.
which was called Tioga, from the river that ran

through its southern part. Chemung Township was situated in this new county, and Newtown was made a half-shire town; that is; a place where courts are held part of the time.

In 1792 a further change came to the locality; the township of Newtown was erected from the Chemung Township. It was very symmetrical in shape; almost a parallelogram; and reached from the Pennsylvania line to Seneca Lake. The first town meeting was held in May of the year named at the same Kline tavern already spoken of.

First Court House.—It was not until four years later, in 1796, that a Court House was built to sustain the dignity of the half shire. It was situated on the east side of Sullivan Street; about half way between Church and Second Streets. It was neither a pretentious nor expensive structure, being built of logs, but it must have been firmly put together; for it served the purpose for which it was erected for thirty years; and remnants of it were observable in very recent times. Courts were held before it was completed; at the same Kline House; and there many of the most distinguished legal lights of the State appeared. The new building; which was two stories and an attic in height, was used for other purposes than the trial of causes. In the lower story was the jail; and the home; sometimes, of the Sheriff and sometimes of an under Sheriff. The court-room itself served as an auditorium for religious services; and in the attic were held the meetings of a Masonic lodge. A lodge of Masons was connected with General Sullivan's army; and this lodge that met in the Court House was chartered

on June 28, 1793; as Union Lodge No. 30. It was
the second lodge of Masons formed in the western
part of the State. Some of the most influential
men of the region were members.

The first school-house was erected about this
time. It also was built of logs, and was in the woods;
standing on a hill; where now stands the Masonic
Temple. Quite contemporary with this was the
school-house built in Horseheads in 1793, its first
teacher being Amelia Parkhurst.

Visiting royalty.—The year 1797 was marked in
the locality by an incident that for a long time was
the subject of local comment and more or less com-
placency. The French Duke of Orleans; who subsequently became King Louis Phillippe; and his
brothers, the Duke de Nemours and the Duke de
Berri, on their way from Canandaigua to the French
emigre settlements on the Susquehanna and Phila-
delphia, tarried for several days at the same Kline
tavern. They had walked all the way from Canandaigua and waited in Elmira until suitable boats
could be prepared to carry them farther on their
journey.

The character of the settlers.—In early times like
these there were few settlers who were professional
men; unless to their profession they added some
trade or calling. In pioneer days carpenters;
workers in leather, blacksmiths; gunsmiths; hatters;
shoemakers, and those of the other useful occupa-
tions were more needed. Almost every farmer
was able to mend; if not make; his farming imple-
ments; which were few and simple; could mend

or make[11] the shoes or boots of his family, and the women of the pioneers could attend to the clothing.

Horseheads and Big Flats.—No stranger ever heard the names of the two townships of Chemung County, Horseheads, and Big Flats, without a smile of bewilderment, that sometimes dwindled into derision. But they are both natural and descriptive names. General Sullivan, on his return, didn't have enough "fodder" for his horses. Rather than have them suffer for food or fall into the hands of the enemy, he killed a number of them where Horseheads is located, and left their bones to bleach in the sunlight. There were enough skulls to identify the locality as a spot where there were so many horse's heads. This very naturally grew

[11]VINCENT MATTHEWS was the first lawyer to settle in the county. He was a man of unusual abilities and was one of the most distinguished citizens of the State of his time. Dr. AMOS PARK was the first physician. But he was more than a physician. He was a teacher and preacher, and built, largely with his own hands, the first frame house in Elmira. Dr. JOSEPH HINCHMAN soon followed Dr. Park. He became a prominent man in the community, was Sheriff of the county for one term, and held other public offices. JOHN BENNETT was a carpenter and joiner, coming into Horseheads from Orange County. His son, COMFORT became the largest landholder in the county. The family was a large one and has many representatives to this day. WILLIAM HOFFMAN, one of the strongest characters of his day, was a hatter. He acquired large wealth and contributed to the county many distinguished sons. WILLIAM DUNN, the original ancestor of the family of that name that became prominent in the valley, was an innkeeper. NATHAN TEALL was an innkeeper. From his youngest daughter Elmira gets its name. He was a conspicuous and active man, and as under sheriff was the first one to occupy and have charge of the new Court House on Sullivan Street. ABRAHAM MILLER, who became the first Judge of the county, was a wagon-maker and blacksmith. His family arose to great prominence in the affairs of the county.

into the name of the place. Big Flats was known to the Indians as "Great Plains." It was descriptive, for the great prairies of the West were unknown then. In the rural vernacular, the dignified Indian appellation dropped into "Big Flats." At best; either name is better than borrowing from the classical dictionary or the countries of Europe.

As we have seen, in a little more than a decade, the last one of the eighteenth century, what is now the county of Chemung acquired a momentum toward development that augured well for the future of the locality.

PART II

—

The County of Chemung during the first half of the XIX Century

—

Ah, happy hills! Ah, pleasing shade!
  Ah, fields beloved in vain!
Where once my careless childhood strayed,
  A stranger yet to pain:
I feel the gales that from ye blow,
A momentary bliss bestow,
As, waving fresh their gladsome wing,
  My weary soul they seem to soothe,
And, redolent of joy and youth,
  To breathe a second spring.—Thomas Gray.

Still o'er these scenes my memory wakes
  And fondly broods with miser care;
Time but the impression deeper makes,
  As streams their channels deeper wear.
                                  —Robert Burns.

The First Half of the XIXth Century

Postal facilities.—The first day of the new century; January 1; 1801; was signalized by the establishment of two new post-offices in the county. At Chemung; Elijah Buck being the postmaster and at Newtown; John Konkle being the postmaster. John Konkle's son; Aaron Konkle; succeeded his father as postmaster in 1809.[12]

The county's first citizens.—Chemung County from the start was fortunate and continues so to be, to the present time; in counting among its citizens men who were untiring in their efforts to advance the prosperity of their locality; and it is to be observed that in different periods the same men always appear united in the one purpose then in view.[13]

---

[12]Elijah Buck served as Postmaster for thirty-three years; Aaron Konkle for thirteen years. He was afterward District-Attorney for the county for nine years, and County Judge for one year. The family name of Konkle, once so prominent, has entirely disappeared from the County.

[13]In this early period, the beginning of the XIXth century, the following-named men seemed to be at the bottom of every public undertaking, all stirring, active citizens: John H. Knapp, Grant B. Baldwin, Samuel H. Maxwell, Levi J. Cooley, John Konkle, Stephen Tuttle, Asahel Buck, John Arnot, Robert Covell, William Guthrie, Dexter Newell, Ebenezer Sayre, Elijah Hinman, Isaac Baldwin, Guy Maxwell, John C. Clark, Abner M. Hetfield, Matthew Carpenter, Solomon L. Smith, William Maxwell, Lyman Covell, David Reynolds, Caleb Baker, John G. McDowell, Alonzo I. Wynkoop, all of whom have left representatives in the valley, and all of whom are remembered with affection and respect.

There were a number of attempts at enterprises which seem now to be curious and ahead of their times; as they never came to anything; showing; however; the activity prevalent.[14]

One of the most eagerly sought-for and desired enterprises was an easier and more rapid method of communication for business purposes with the people of the State to which the county belonged; and not to be so utterly dependent upon the river and the States of Pennsylvania and Maryland.

Methods of communication with the outer world.— On March 22, 1803, an act of the Legislature was procured; authorizing the construction of a turnpike from Newtown to Seneca Lake; to connect there with the turnpike to Catskill on the Hudson. This was the beginning of what is now known as Lake Street; in Elmira; and it ran from the Chemung River to the head of the lake at "Catherine's Landing," now Watkins.

Then authority was given to certain ones to ex-

---

[14]There was a corporation authorized in the first decade of the century called "The Tioga Coal, Iron, and Manufacturing Company." It had a very wide sweep of operations. It was authorized to dig and vend coal, and manufacture iron and glass. It went much farther than this, for the corporation was allowed to do whatever it chose with the Chemung River; build towpaths, locks, culverts, dams, anything to improve the stream. It was also authorized to lay a railroad to the Pennsylvania line. There was a "Chemung Mutual Insurance Company" that never wrote a policy, and a "Chemung and Ithaca Railroad" that contemplated, but never built, a line down Wynkoop Creek, also to the Pennsylvania line. In the latter part of the year 1829, there was a company incorporated with very ample powers called "The Seneca and Susquehanna Lock Navigation Company." It surrendered its rights, however, in favor of the Chemung Canal.

plore[15] and lay out a route to connect Ithaca, then in Seneca County, with Newtown.

In 1807, the only regular communication by mail that the county had was with Wilkesbarre, Pa., by means of a post-boy on horseback, who took four days for the journey, each way, a distance of hardly one hundred miles.[16]

The Chemung Canal.—The chief and most important result of the efforts of the county at this period was the construction of the Chemung Canal.[17] Judge Caleb Baker, of Chemung Township, at the time Member of Assembly for the county, was largely instrumental in carrying the bill through to its successful conclusion.[18]   When it was known

---

[15]The word "explore," used in the act, was particularly apt and expressive. This was in 1812, and at that time and as late as 1823, the State was offering a reward of five dollars each for the destruction of any "wolf or wolf-whelp or panther" in the County of Tioga, in which Chemung was situated, and two dollars each for wild-cats!

[16]The community was always in need of iron and nails. It is curious now to read how it got them. In 1827, PHILIP SCHULTZ, assisted by his brother John, was doing the work as occasion required. They had a great canvas-covered wagon like a "prairie schooner," drawn by four horses, and plied between Elmira and Bellefonte, Pa. Each trip occupied from two to three weeks, and the return was almost as much of an event to the village as when a ship comes in.

[17]The first steps were taken by the Legislature looking to the work on April 25, 1825, when the selection of a suitable route from the river to Seneca Lake was authorized. The undertaking was made certain on April 15, 1829, by the appropriation of $300,000 for the construction of the work. It is to be observed that this act, for the first time, gave the official designation of the river as "The Chemung." Before this it had been called "The Tioga River."

[18]Judge BAKER was a conspicuous citizen of the county in those early days, active, and enterprising. He came to the locality in 1798. He, through his son-in-law, Richard A. Baker, who was a prominent politician in his day, left many

that the bill had passed, there was great rejoicing
all through the region that the canal traversed.
Work was begun in 1830, with impressive cere-
monies, Col. John Hendy throwing up the first
spadeful of earth, and when it was completed in
1832, a similar; if not wilder, celebration was in-
dulged in; in which appeared a barge, loaded down
to suffocation; drawn by four horses, and profusely
decorated with American flags; with the same Col.
John Hendy standing proudly at the prow "sail-
ing up" the stream as far as Millport.⁹   Not a vestige of this public work now remains.

Stage-coaching days.—Stage-coaching in the valley during the last three decades of the half century
was an important and rather picturesque interest.
There were lines established from Elmira to the
head of Seneca Lake, down the river to Owego,
Binghamton; and Wilkesbarre, south to Williamsport; Pa., and up the river to Corning and Bath.
Handsome Concord coaches; drawn by well-kept
four-horse teams, were used and they enlivened the
landscape as they moved on; with pleasant effect.
The first coach ever run in the valley was to "Cath-

---

descendants who became some of the best-known citizens
of the county.

¹⁹This little village, originally "Millvale," became of much
note by reason of its abundance of water-power. It is near
the summit of the streams, one flowing south, toward the
Chemung River, and the other north into Seneca Lake.   It
speedily had numerous sawmills in operation, and a number
of boat-building yards. The first two boats were built by
JOHN JACKSON, a lively citizen of Horseheads, and were
named by him *General Sullivan* and *Lady Sullivan*. They
were launched on the Fourth of July of the year subsequent
to the opening of the canal.

erine's Landing,"[20] at the head of Seneca Lake. It
was run by John Davis, whose inn at the corner of
what is now Lake and East Water Streets, in Elmira,
"The Black Horse Tavern," was for many years
the most conspicuous spot in the valley; the place
for all public gatherings of every kind that were
held.[21]

The Erie Railway.—On April 21; 1825; an act
was passed by the Legislature ordering a survey to
be made through the southern tier of New York
to discover a route for a railroad, and the line now
in operation and existence was declared to be im-
practicable!

Nevertheless; seven years later; on April 24; 1832,
the organization of the "New York and Erie Railroad Company" was authorized by the Legislature;
realizing the hopes and expectations of every citizen of the county to get into complete, easy; and
close communication with the whole world.

The road was completed to Elmira in the fall of
1849.[22]

On April 21; 1832; the Legislature authorized the

-----

[20]This little place, not now in Chemung County, got its
original name from the fact there was located there an Indian
village owned by "Catherine Montour," the half-breed wife
of a Seneca Chief.

[21]Those who controlled these early lines of travel were
J. Davis Baldwin, Sly, and McGrath, and Cooley and Maxwell, all public-spirited and active citizens.

[22]The first Superintendent of the division of the road in
which Chemung County is situated was William E. Rutter,
an experienced railroad man who came from Providence,
R. I.   His eldest son, James H. Rutter, became the President of the New York Central & Hudson River Railroad.
Another Superintendent of the division in later years was
H. D. V. Pratt, who achieved high distinction as a railroad
man, becoming the General Superintendent of the road.

construction of a railroad from Elmira to Williamsport; Pa., but advantage was not taken of its pro-
visions until twenty years later.

On May 14; 1845, the Chemung Railroad Company
was incorporated. Its line was from Elmira to
Seneca Lake. The Erie road used it to make con-
nections; by means of the Lake [23] at Geneva, with
the railroad already established there.

Commercial enterprises.—The building of the
canal had given a powerful impulse to the business
of the county. Every town had felt it.[24] The
chief product of the county was lumber; of which
the white pine; in width and quality, has never
been equalled in the markets of the country. There
were sawmills established in every corner and mil-
lions of feet found an easy market; by means of
the canal.[25]

---

[23]It was an era in steamboating on the interior lakes of
the State. The *Ben Loder*, named for the President of the
Erie road, in size and equipment would compare favorably
with the best boats anywhere. It was long remembered
in the locality with satisfaction and pride. Nothing equaling it has since been seen there.

[24]The town of Horseheads perhaps had felt it the most.
In three years it nearly doubled in population. It seemed
to be the most important village on the canal, being at the
junction of the "feeder" to the canal, coming from the
upper waters of the river near Corning. The tolls were col-
lected there and the office for their collection was maintained
there for forty-three years. Thomas Maxwell was the first
collector. Soon after the opening of the canal, on May 15,
1837, the village was incorporated as "Fairport." It was
well enough for it was very fair and a sure enough "port,"
if an inland one. But the people wouldn't have it. They
stood it for eight years, but with much discontent and grum-
bling, and on April 8, 1845, they were glad to get back to the
honest, descriptive old Saxon "Horseheads." It is likely
it will ever remain so.

[25]In the town of Southport, advantage being taken of

A large number of persons engaged in the lumber traffic came to the county very soon after the opening of the canal.[26]

There were many woolen mills scattered through the county. The first one was established in the town of Southport by Silas Billings, in 1820. Another one, and the largest in the county, was built in 1842, on Newtown Creek, at the foot of East Hill, Elmira, by Daniel and Ransom Pratt, brothers.[27]

The purely mercantile men who were attracted to the county during this period by its growing

---

Seely and South Creeks, from 1840 to 1844, there were eighteen sawmills in operation. "Pine City," in the township originally "Pine Woods," a little hamlet, owes its name to its chief product. Charles Atkins, a cooper by trade, the first settler there, came in 1830. Pine Valley, in Veteran Township, where the supply of white pine was also large, gets its name from the same source.

[26]Among those deserving to be remembered were the following-named, who attained high positions in the business world of the county, and occupied conspicuous positions in other lines than that in which they were particularly engaged. Samuel B. Strang, Benjamin A. Towner, Asaph Colburn, Lyman Gibson, William S. Hatch, Henry M. Partridge, Bradley Griffin, J. C. Sampson, Hiram Crane, W. E. Judson, Aaron F. Potter, William L. Gibson, Andrus and Langdon, Richmond Jones, Ward Jones, James Fairman, Henry C. Spaulding, William Halliday, William Birdsall, and the four Fitch Brothers, D. H., O. N., John S., and Lewis. Some of these, after the supply of lumber was exhausted, sought other fields and pastures new, but most of them engaged in other pursuits in the city.

[27]DANIEL and RANSOM PRATT were Scotchmen. They tried the neighborhood of the upper part of the county, but came to the spot they had selected in the year named. The water-power furnished by Newtown Creek was fine. They were the first to introduce into the county the power loom and wool-condensing machines. They were very successful in their undertakings, and in time founded the Second National Bank in Elmira.

importance, were numerous. Many of their "stores" seemed to be the originals of what are now called "department stores," for they carried in stock about everything from kid gloves to grindstones.[28]

Circulating medium.—Business, as it was increasing, called for some circulating medium. Much, if not all, of the traffic was carried on by barter, a system that at the time was taught in the district schools, very much to the annoyance, if not displeasure, of the children. The products of the soil were valuable and plentiful, but men needed something besides a wagon load of wheat or a bin of oats with which to pay their debts. This need gave rise to the incorporation of the Chemung

---

[28]It is a long list, for they were many, and going over it is like striking the chords of a harp that has long been mute. There is not in all the county a single name left of all those that made up the business community in the first half of last century. Here they are, and every one of them has an interest for some one who will recall them with pleasure and often with affection: David H. Tuthill, Benjamin C. Wickham, Matthew McReynolds, Joseph Dumars, S. S. ᴊuce, S. B. Hubbell, J. M. Robinson, Robert and Edward Covell, Miles Covell, William Viall, Norris North, E. L. Skinner, Green M. Tuthill, Timothy Satterlee, William Foster, George Kingsbury, John Selover, R. F. Seabury, James Reeves, John Parmenter, D. A. Towner, Brinton Paine, Solomon L. Gillett, William Hoffman, Wakeman Merwin, Riggs Watrous, G. A. Gridley, S. S. Hamlin, R. C. Rice, J. K. Perry, John Hill, David Bulmer, John N. Elmore, T. O. Elmore, William P. Yates, Samuel Hall, Samuel Partridge, William Ogden, Tracy Beadle, Simeon Benjamin, Anson C. Ely, Francis Hall, Christopher Preswick, A. Z. Sickles, James T. Dudley, Stephen Hill, Erastus Hill, Henry Wilson, Edward Maxwell, William E. Hart, Seth Kelly, Elijah Jones, Noah Robinson, H. M. Seward, Fox Holden, E. P. Hutchinson, H. D. Treadwell, Stephen McDonald, John R. Jones, the Hanfords (boot and shoe men), Platt Cole, F. A. Scribner, E. S. Palmer, Thomas S. Pattinson, George Pattinson, Ephraim P. Davenport, William McClure, Christian Smith.

Canal Bank.[29]   Its first president was John G.
McDowell,[30] and its first cashier, William Maxwell.[31]   In 1842 the bank came under the control
of John Arnot[32] and so remained for many years.

The Bank of Chemung was organized in 1849.
Its first president was Simeon Benjamin, and its
first cashier, Tracy Beadle.[33]

---

[29]Its charter was obtained on April 9, 1833. Subscrip-
tions were asked for the stock, and although only $200,000
was required, there were received offers that amounted to
$1,434,450. For more than seventy years it stood a finan-
cial rock upon which the whole neighborhood rested in
security and content.

[30]Judge JOHN G. McDOWELL was one of the most remarkable men produced in the county. He was the son of Daniel
McDowell, one of the first settlers of the valley, and was
born in 1794, in Chemung Township. He took a large part
in the War of 1812, and was an intimate personal friend of
all the eminent men of his day. He was a member of Assembly for one term, State Senator, and one of the old Commissioners of Loans. He was a presidential elector in 1852,
voting for the successful candidate. It was his last appearance in public life. Descendants of his are yet among the
most highly-esteemed citizens of the county.

[31]WILLIAM MAXWELL was a son of Guy Maxwell, who came
early to the valley, and in his time occupied a very high position in all the affairs of the county. He was State Senator
for one term. Some of the blood of the Maxwells remain
in the valley, but not more than one or two of the name.

[32]JOHN ARNOT stands alone in the annals of the county, a
colossal figure of business and finance. He was a Scotchman, born at Perthshire in 1789. He came to the valley
in 1819, on a mercantile venture, and remained there. From
that time all his life was passed there. All his enterprises
were successful, and he amassed a fortune of great magnitude, which he dispensed with rare judgment and generosity.
His wife was the granddaughter of Matthias Hollenback.
He died in 1873. But one life remains to perpetuate his
name, and when that is gone it will become only a memory.

[33]SIMEON BENJAMIN came to Elmira from Long Island in
1833. He was at the time possessed of considerable wealth
and for many years after his settlement in Elmira was
esteemed the richest man there. He had great business
capacity and largely "increased his store." He was also a

Matters pertaining to religion.—The Presbyterian
Church in Elmira, the "old Mother Church" as it
has been called, of the county in the early part of
the century, was in charge of the Rev. Simeon Jones,
who came to the county from New Jersey in 1804.
He was also a school teacher and united the two
professions in one.³⁴   There is a long list of eminent
clergymen who faithfully served this First Church.³⁵

The first feeble beginnings of a Presbyterian
Church were made in Southport in 1820.   In
Horseheads the first Presbyterian Church of the
town was organized on February 8, 1832.   It was
effected under the charge of the Revs. Ethan Pratt,
M. L. Farnsworth, and Elder John McConnell.
The first church edifice was erected in 1832.   In

generous and liberal man, making the Elmira College for
Women possible by his large gifts to it in the early days of
its existence.

TRACY BEADLE was a druggist, coming to Elmira from
Cooperstown, N. Y., in 1835. With everything that the words
imply he was indeed, always one of the leading citizens of
the valley, meriting the title "A Christian Gentleman."

³⁴The Rev. SIMEON JONES was followed into the valley by
three brothers.   Joel was a tailor, who settled in Southport.
Elijah was a jeweler, who, however, became an innkeeper
and for many years was in charge of the "Mansion House"
in Elmira, and made it a well-known hostelry all over that
portion of the State.   Philo settled in 1817 in the town of
Southport, and became one of its best-known and popular
citizens.   For seventeen years he was the proprietor of a
hotel in the locality where he had settled.   He built mills
and further improved the country thereabouts, and served
one term as Member of Assembly.   A son of his, Finla M.
Jones, served as postmaster at the little hamlet where he
lived, for twenty-seven years.

³⁵Among those well remembered are Dr. Philomon H.
Fowler, who served eleven years, and was at one time the
Moderator of the General Assembly, and Dr. David Murdoch,
a Scotchman, strong, hearty, and patient.   One of his sons,
John Murdoch, became one of the most distinguished mem-
bers of the Chemung County Bar.

Big Flats the first Presbyterian Church was organized in 1825, with Nathan Reynolds, Charles Fry, and Joseph Pound as deacons. In 1829 an edifice was built. Its first settled pastor was the Rev. S. Harmon. In Veteran, at the village of Millport, a church was organized in 1836, Myron Collins and Jervis Langdon[36] being active in the undertaking. The Rev. H. L. Jackson was the first pastor. By the removal of many prominent families the society became disorganized and its church became the property of the Baptists. In Erin a Presbyterian Church was erected in 1836, but after a few years the society disbanded.

From early in the century there had been occasionally a Methodist minister who, riding his circuit, had found the little spot on the Chemung and had ministered as he was able to those of his faith. It was not, however, until 1812 that the town was regularly included in a Methodist circuit. The first class was organized in 1819, and the first class leader was Isaac Roe.[37] The first Sunday-school

---

[36]JERVIS LANGDON was one of the most prominent and highly thought of citizens of the county. He attained a very high position in the business world of the county. Almost his first business adventure was made in Millport, where he came in 1838, when less than thirty years of age. The place was small, but there was great activity there on account of the recent opening of the Chemung Canal. It may be remembered that it aspired to be the rival of Elmira in business importance and population. MYRON COLLINS, spoken of, was MR. LANGDON's partner. MR. LANGDON came to Elmira in 1845, and ever after, until his death, resided there. He achieved a great success in the coal trade, being the first one to introduce anthracite in the Western country. One of his daughters became the wife of S. L. Clemens (Mark Twain).

[37]ISAAC ROE came to the valley in 1817. His wife was a Drake, of the same family as the famous Sir Francis Drake.

of the church was organized in 1825; and the first
church building was erected in 1832.[35] Many eminent men of the church in their turn had charge
of this society during the first half of the century,
and under their ministrations it prospered to a
great degree.[39]

He was a tanner and shoemaker by trade. A son of his,
Francis A., was an officer in the American navy, and rose
to the rank of Rear-Admiral. He died in January, 1902.

A strong member of this church in those early days was
John Hughes, an Irish Catholic, and one of the Irish "1798
patriots." He came to Newtown in 1803, and became a
Methodist. He was, without doubt, the first Irishman to
settle in the valley. He did so much for the church that
he was affectionately called and remembered as "Father
Hughes." One of his sons, George, born in Newtown, was
an officer in the United States Army, and made a gallant
record in the Mexican War. Another son, Aaron Konkle,
named for his uncle, the son of John Konkle, was an officer
in the United States Navy, served in the Civil War, and
became a Rear-Admiral.

[38]A pathetic incident connected with the building of the
church has a melancholy interest in the annals of the Society.
John Kline, a son of Isaac Roe, mentioned, was preparing
himself for the ministry. He fell sick at the institution
where he was studying, and died. He was brought home
to Elmira to be buried, and the funeral services were held
in the yet unfinished church. They were the first services
of any kind held in the building, and a carpenter's bench
was used for a pulpit and a bier. The circumstance had an
impressive effect, and a revival followed that gave a great
impetus toward the upbuilding of the church.

A well-remembered member of the church, Elias S. Hunt-
ley, who came to Elmira in 1828, made a remarkable record
in the service of the church. For sixty-four years he was
a class leader, and for nineteen years the Sunday-School
superintendent.

[39]Some of these deserve to be recalled. The Rev. John
N. Maffit, a famous evangelist, made a number of visits, and
his revivals were very greatly blessed. In the year 1823
came to the church the Rev. Edmund O'Flyng, a peculiar
man, full of eccentric actions and speeches. The raftsmen
of the period might be called picturesque in their profanity.
Once one of these vessels on which he was riding somewhat
for pleasure, more to try and reach the attention of some

The Methodist Church in the township of Chemung had its origin in a revival in 1819. There
was a class of thirty members. The first meeting
was held in an old log school-house, the first resident pastor being the Rev. William H. Pearne. In
1849 the present church was built and occupied in
1850. In Horseheads the Methodists depended
on Elmira for their church privileges, and one was
not organized there until 1839. John Vaughan
held meetings at Pine Valley in Veteran Township,
in 1825, but there was no society organized until
1858. Local preachers held meetings in the township of Erin earlier than 1828, but there was no
organization until long after.

Baptists were early in the field. A society was
formed on May 16, 1829, called the Southport and
Elmira Baptist Church. In 1831, it was legally
recognized and became the "Baptist organization
of the towns of Southport and Elmira." The early

---

of the men, got entangled in a jam.   The event unbottled
the speech of the raftsmen and it flowed out with unusual
volubility.   Mr. O'Flyng was greatly disturbed by it, and
referring to it afterward averred that he thought they were
all "going to hell by water!"   His eccentricities annoyed the
conference, and once he was given a sharp reprimand by the
bishop.   Nevertheless he was eloquent and popular, and
retained the charge for four years.   In 1834 came to the
church the Rev. Allen Steele.   His son, who became Dr.
J. Dorman Steele, arose to great distinction as an author of
school text-books, achieved a national, if not an European,
reputation, becoming one of the most distinguished scholars
of his day, in whom and whose memory the country has a
right to take great pride.

As showing the method pursued in those old times in
building churches, it might be stated that on a subscription
list, still extant, appears not much money but twenty perch
of stone, value $120, from one; 1,000 feet of lumber from
another; and from others store goods, $20; blacksmithing,
$5; hats, $10; teaming, $10.

church was indebted to the labors of the Rev. P. D. Gillette, who formed other organizations throughout the county, and to Jeffery Wisner, who gave the plot of ground on which the church was built in 1830.

Baptist preachers came to Horseheads as early as 1805. In 1827 a church was erected about two miles north of the village. About April 22, 1840; a church was organized which in the latter part of the year united with the Elmira organization and was known as "The Elmira and Fairport Church." A church edifice was erected in 1841. In Big Flats a church was organized on August 30, 1807. The first services were held in a barn, and then in schoolhouses. The Rev. Roswell Goff was the first pastor. A church edifice was built in 1827, and occupied in January, 1828. The Ridge Free Baptist church was organized in Veteran, November 19; 1836. The first pastor was the Rev. Samuel Dean.

The beginnings of the Episcopal Church were made in 1833, a clergyman coming to the village of Elmira and holding services in a school-house.[40]

---

[40]Among its rectors were the Rev. Andrew Hull, who served as such seventeen years; the Rev. B. W. Whitcher, whose wife wrote the celebrated "Widow Bedott Papers," and the Rev. William Paret, who became the Bishop of Maryland. One of the characters of the early times who had much to do in organizing the church, was "Aunty Hill," a Protestant Irish woman, who kept a garden in the western part of the village. She herself went to Trinity Church, New York City, and secured a contribution sufficient to justify the beginning in 1840 of the Trinity Church. Hervey Luce was a very active man in organizing the church. He was a hatter. He served as Senior Warden for many years. His son-in-law, the Hon. William T. Post, became a prominent man. He served one term as Member of Assembly and was postmaster of the village of Elmira four years.

The Church was regularly organized on March 31, 1834.

St. Paul's Episcopal Church was organized in Big Flats in 1830, and an edifice erected in 1834. The first rector was the Rev. E. T. Gilbert. The church became partially disorganized in 1843, services being held occasionally by rectors from Corning and Elmira.[41]

During the time of the construction of the canal a number of those connected with and attached to the Roman Catholic faith came into the valley, many taking up their residences and making their homes in the county. These were ministered to by priests from other places. In 1848 was begun a small but convenient wooden chapel where now stands the church of SS. Peter and Paul, at High and Market Streets, Elmira. Father Sheridan was the first resident pastor.

Burial places.—Very early in the century the subject of locations where the dead could be laid away called for attention. On many of the farms throughout the county are still to be seen by the roadside or under the trees some distance therefrom; well kept always and surrounded by white palings; small plots of ground in which are standing headstones bearing dates very early in the last century as well as more recent ones. Whether or not any of the families of the early settlers occupy the lands about, it is not at all likely that these sacred spots will ever be disturbed.

[41] The Tuttle family was largely interested in this church. one of its members, the Rev. Daniel S. Tuttle, becoming the Bishop of Missouri and the presiding bishop of his church.

The first public cemetery was located nearly at
the corner of what is now East Water and Sullivan
Streets; in Elmira. Long since; every vestige of
the existence of such a spot there disappeared, and
it is said that the bodies were never removed therefrom. Very recently, in excavating for the founda-
tions of a large manufacturing establishment; the
location of this ancient burying-ground was dis-
covered. In 1802 Jeffrey Wisner gave the land
for a cemetery where Wisner Park is now located;
on Main Street; in Elmira. In 1838 the Second
Street cemetery was opened, and that is now occasionally used.

Big Flats also early provided for a public burial-
ground. In 1809 a plot of land was set apart for
the purpose. The first burials therein were Amos
Rowley; who died on June 5, 1809, and Robert
Miller, who died on July 14, 1809.

Public houses and halls.—Tradition; with little of
memory or record to sustain it, is always busy with
the public houses of any locality. For many reasons they are the most prominent spots in any town;
new or old, and what they are is often taken to be
what the town itself is. Away down on Water
Street; in Elmira, was located the first public house
or tavern in the county. No one knows the exact
spot upon which it stood. Not a vestige of it
remains. Then there were the "Kline House"
and "The Black Horse Tavern," already spoken of.
The two Mansion Houses, at different times and in
different locations, and the "Elmira Hotel,"[42] built

[42]Among the landlords controlling the destinies of this
hostelry was Henry Potter, who came from Rensselaer

on the banks of the canal soon after its completion. There was the old "Eagle Tavern," which burned in 1849, and was succeeded by the "Brainard." The inns contained the halls used for balls and for entertainments, theatrical and musical. There were other halls, "Temperance Hall," "Mechanics Hall," Pattinson[43] Hall, and Concert Hall.

Determining more geographical divisions.—There was much shifting and changing as regards the townships in the early part of the century. On April 6, 1808, a portion was taken from Chemung Township, made into another township, and called Elmira.[44] The name applied to the township, not to the village which remained Newtown until April 21, 1828, when it, too, became Elmira. Another township called Erin was sliced away from Chemung Township on March 29, 1822. The first

County, N. Y. He held the place from 1839 to 1848. He held a number of offices both in civil and military life. His oldest son was William C. Potter, who possessed many extraordinary qualities, chief of which was his talent for painting. Some of his portraits possessed great merit. He died at the early age of thirty-four, having hardly begun his life.

[43]In the hall of the Elmira house mentioned was given the first dramatic representation ever undertaken in the valley, the company being that of Gilbert and Trobridge. The Gilbert was John Gilbert, who afterward attained great distinction in his profession.

The Pattinson brothers, Thomas and George, were merchants. They were descended from the famous George Stevenson, who invented the locomotive.

[44]The name is said to be derived from the Spanish, El Mira, "the view," or "the fine view." It was brought into the language by one of the early English novelists of the 18th century. It was the name of a daughter of Nathan Teall, who kept the tavern where Judge Coryell, the Member of Assembly, always stopped, and he was very fond of the child.

town meeting was held in May at the house of John
Bandfield.⁴⁵ In April of the same year the township of Elmira suffered two losses. A strip on the
north became the township of Big Flats, and on
the south the township of Southport.⁴⁶ Still further,
on April 16, 1823, two more townships were formed
from the southern end of Catherine; Veteran on the
east half and Catlin on the west half. Veteran was
named in honor of a revolutionary soldier, Green
Bentley, and Catlin from Phineas Catlin, an active,
energetic man, a farmer with some knowledge of
surveying.⁴⁷ The northern half of Catlin was, on April
17, 1835, taken to form another township named
Dix, after Gen. John A. Dix. And then the divid-
ing, for the time being, ceased.

Another Court House.—In 1824 the new Court
House was built on Lake Street in Elmira to take

⁴⁵One of the strong names of the county. This one mentioned was at one time Member of Assembly.

⁴⁶Its first town meeting was held on May 14, 1822. Solomon L. Smith was the first Supervisor, and he served in that
capacity for five years. John Wormly was an early settler
in the township and was active in its affairs. By his efforts
the first school-house was erected there in in 1838.

⁴⁷What was left of the Township of Catherine is now in
Schuyler County. The village of Millport is in the Township
of Veteran. It grew very rapidly on the completion of
the Chemung Canal. A. F. Babcock, a stirring politician of
the county, was a merchant there many years, and became
County Clerk. The county is also indebted to the township
and village for the Hon. Gabriel L. Smith, who at first prac-
ticed law in Millport with Judge Theodore North as partner.
for five years, and then came to Elmira. He was a prominent officer in the Civil War, and became County Judge.
He celebrated the sixtieth anniversary of his wedding day on
November 7, 1904, and died two years later at the advanced
age of 84 years. The county and State are also indebted to
this township for another able lawyer, the Hon. Sylvester S.
Taylor, who was District-Attorney of the County, County
Judge, and an Assistant Attorney-General of the State.

the place of the old one on Sullivan Street. It was esteemed quite a pretentious building and commanded the admiration of all. It served its purpose for almost forty years.

At last, the new county.—All this was looking toward an important and distinctive event; the formation of the county of Chemung. This was accomplished by act of the Legislature of March 29, 1836. It comprised the following-named townships: Chemung, Elmira, Big Flats, Erin, Southport, Catlin, Veteran, Catherine, Cayuta, and Dix.[48] The first Assemblyman for the county was Jacob Westlake, of Horseheads; the first District-Attorney, Andrew K. Gregg; the first County Judge, Joseph L. Darling; the first County Clerk, Isaac Baldwin; the first Sheriff, A. A. Becknith. Hiram Gray[49] was the first Congressman taken from the county. The population of the new county was 17,465.

---

[48]The three last named are now a part of Schuyler County and form no part of this story.

The first Supervisors of the county were: Big Flats, Samuel Minier; Catlin, Timothy Wheat; Cayuta, Jacob Swartwood; Catherine, John G. Henry; Chemung, Isaac Shepherd; Dix, Green Bennett; Elmira, John W. Wisner; Erin, Robert Stewart; Southport, Albert A. Beckwith; Veteran, Asahel Hulett.

[49]HIRAM GRAY was doubtless the most eminent jurist ever produced by the county. He came to Elmira in 1825, from Washington County, N. Y., and remained one of the foremost citizens of the valley for more than sixty years. He held many official positions in the county, city, and State. serving a term in the Supreme Court of the district, and on the Commission of Appeals of the State. He died in 1890.

This period developed in the county many lawyers of ability and learning, enjoying, as they had earned, a State reputation. Some of these not elsewhere mentioned were: Theodore North, Jr., Elijah P. Brooks, Erastus P. Hart,

The river.—The river was always, in these early days, the most attractive, interesting and valuable portion of the valley. On its swollen waters in the spring and fall were borne the rafts and arks that bore the lumber and produce of the locality to a market at Baltimore, Md. The beauty spot of the valley was a large island almost two miles in extent that lay just in front of Elmira. It was covered with primeval trees, and had a profuse green turf. Here it was that picnics assembled and gatherings of all sorts celebrated festal days.[50] No effort was made to preserve the spot in its pristine loveliness, and it is now a mere waste of sand and gravel uncomfortable to look at.[51]

One of the earliest thoughts about the river was how to get over on the other side. Steps were begun in 1817 to build a bridge at Elmira, but the effort had no fruition until seven years later, and it was not until 1824 that the first bridge was thrown over the stream at Elmira. The second one was built the next year, near the village of Chemung.

Solomon B. Tomlinson, E. H. Benn, James L. Woods, John W. Wisner, William H. Patterson, James Dunn, Peter Van Der Lyn, Ariel S. Thurston, Thomas G. Spaulding, who served as County Judge for ten years, Edward Quinn, James A. Christie, H. Boardman Smith, Archibald Robertson, Aaron Konkle, Newton P. Fassett.

[50]Anson C. Ely, one of the most active merchants of the time, offered to contribute $10,000 toward the preservation of the spot, but there were no other persons found to second him in his endeavor.

[51]As showing the large amount of trade carried on on the river, it may be stated, as a matter of record, that in the spring of 1829 there were sent down nineteen arks loaded with wheat, carrying 1,800 bushels each, in all 35,000 bushels, and that representing only one interest. It seems small figures now, but then!

The next thought was to make the current useful for driving mills in the building of dams. It was a curious idea the public had in opposing such projects on the ground that it "obstructed navigation." Nevertheless, on January 27, 1824, Isaac Baldwin[52] was given authority by the Legislature to construct a dam opposite the foot of what is now College Avenue. It was not, however, completed until 1828.[53] Two years before, in 1826, Asa and Isaac Parshall had constructed a dam just below the village of Chemung. It was the first one built in the valley. Another one was built in 1827, at Big Flats, by David Reynolds, near his own land.

Strong organizations.—An organization called the "Elmira Mechanics' Society," extraordinary because of its methods and its vitality, was formed in 1834, and was regularly incorporated on May 26, 1836. It was somewhat after the order of the present day "Building Associations." There were fifty mem-

---

[52]Isaac Baldwin was easily one of the first men in the valley all through this period. He was a member of a large and active family that did very much to improve the valley and the county. His home, standing where the Rathbun House is now located, was one of the most notable residences in the county, his farm extending far to the north. His name, attached to the street that was a road through his fields, vividly recalls his memory.

Another one of the family was a distinct character by himself, Waterman Baldwin. He was one of Washington's most trusted scouts, a great hunter and Indian fighter. He had a favorite and famous horse which he named "Roanoke," and for whose use Washington gave a silver mounted saddle. Once each year, and until Washington died, Waterman dined with the General at Mount Vernon.

[53]In the spring following the construction of this work occurred the most destructive ice freshet ever known in the valley. It swept away the dam and covered the fields for

bers, almost entirely made up of carpenters, saddle and harnessmakers, tailors,[54] hatters, blacksmiths, and members of other callings and trades. The society built, in 1840, the first public hall in the valley, and established therein the first public library. It was a large wooden building. It burned in 1866, and was never rebuilt.[55]

Medical.—The Chemung County Medical Society was organized on May 3, 1836. Its first president was Dr. Leonard Hudson. Dr. Nathaniel Aspin-

---

miles about with huge cakes of ice, remnants of which were to be seen in retired spots for months. Numbers felt that it was a judgment on the builders for "obstructing navigation."

[54]Its first officers were: Charles Orwan, a gunsmith, president; Abram Riker, a carpenter, vice-president; Ransom Birdsall, a printer, secretary; Francis Collingwood, a jeweler, treasurer. Some of the Society's officers made remarkable records. John C. Roe, a tailor, was a director for thirty-three years. Josiah Bartholomew, a carpenter, served as president twenty-one years. James S. French served as treasurer for twenty-two years, dying on May 4, 1881, long past his eightieth year.

[55]The strength of a community lies in its workingmen, the producers, and as such the names of those who contributed in large measure during this period toward the upbuilding of the valley, deserve to be recalled. Here are some: Abram Riker, a carpenter and the largest building contractor in the county. He acquired much wealth. He gave the land on which the first Methodist Church was built. He was of the family of the famous Recorder Riker, of New York City. Samuel Jones, Robert F. Hylen, Joseph P. Burt, Josiah Dunham, David Wightman, Jabez Beers, all carpenters, William Williams, a tanner, Job A. Smith, printer, Daniel Stephens, blacksmith, Archibald Heggie, hatter, Francis Smith, saddler, and harnessmaker, Peter Ten Broeck, a wagonmaker, Robert Hill, also a wagonmaker, R. K. Wallace, painter, P. A. La France and Washington Marsh, also painters, Norris North, tinner, Ephraim P. Davenport, tinner, D. S. Hamilton, jeweler, W. B. Berry, shoemaker, Seth Kelly, baker.

wall was its second president, and then[56] came Dr. Erastus L. Hart.[57]

Looking out for fires.—The protection provided against fires was in all hamlets and villages very meager and primitive. They had "bucket brigades," every householder being obliged by law to have on his premises a vessel long and slender made of leather. When there was a fire two lines were formed from the source of supply of water to the flames. One line passed the full buckets along to the fire, and the other line passed the empty buckets to the water. In 1830, Miles Covell, John Arnot, and Abram Riker were made "fire wardens" of the village of Newtown, and soon after a number of the most prominent citizens were named as "firemen of the village." In May, 1834, a fire-engine of a very primitive pattern, called "Old Goose Neck," was purchased, and a company formed to man it. It was known as "Torrent Fire Company, No. 1." A Hook and Ladder Company was organized in 1844, and Fire Company No. 2, called the "Neptune Company," was formed the

---

[56]The medical faculty in the county has long stood very high in the profession, not only in the county, but throughout the State. Among those very useful at this period were Dr. Theseus Brooks, Dr. John Payne, Dr. P. P. Concklin, Dr. Jotham Purdy, Dr. Hollis S. Chubbuck, Dr Nelson Winton, Dr. William Woodward, Dr. Uriah Smith, Dr. D. A. Towner, Dr. Elias Satterlee, Dr. Rulandus Bancroft, Dr. Nathan Boynton.

[57]Dr. Hart was probably the most highly thought of physician of his time in the valley. He came to Elmira from Connecticut in 1823. He was very public-spirited and especially interested in educational matters. His son, William E. Hart, was one of the most enterprising merchants in Elmira for many years, and another son, Erastus P. Hart, became a lawyer of large practice and great distinction.

same year. "Fire Company No. 3," known as the
Red Rover Company, was organized on August 21,
1848. Its first foreman was John I. Nicks.[58] These
companies formed the "Elmira Volunteer Fire
Department." Silas Haight[59] was the first Chief
Engineer of the Fire Department.

How the county got its news.—The county was
always well provided with newspapers. The first
one printed within its borders was called *The Telegraph*, and published in 1815 by Prindle and Murphy.
Its name was changed to the *Vidette*. It struggled
along with such a name until 1816, one year, and
then gave it up. In 1820 the Elmira *Weekly
Republican* was started, but its name was changed
in 1828 to the Elmira *Whig*, and in 1829 it was
called the Elmira *Republican and Canal Advertiser*.
The Elmira *Gazette* was first started in 1820 by
Job A. Smith; a member of a numerous family, and
he called it *The Investigator*. After two years he
changed the name to the Tioga *Register;* and in
1828 to the Elmira *Gazette*. It still exists under

---

[58]MR. NICKS came to Newtown from Dutchess County,
N. Y., in 1847. He was a tobacconist by trade. He became
one of the most enterprising and popular citizens of the
county, known far and wide as a generous, hearty man.
He was very prominent during the Civil War. He served
as Alderman a number of years, was Mayor of the city, State
Senator, and an Internal Revenue Assessor.

[59]MR. HAIGHT was one of the early merchants of the valley.
He came to Elmira in 1836. He subsequently became an
innkeeper, having in his charge the old "Mansion House,"
on Lake Street, the old "Eagle Tavern," and then back to
the same location on Lake Street he had occupied, where he
built an inn called "Haight's Hotel," a famous hostelry
with a State-wide reputation. In his capacity as landlord
for which he was especially fitted, he won and kept the
regard of all the citizens of the county.

that name, having passed a long career of honor and prosperity. The Chemung *Democrat* was started in 1847. In 1831 there were two peculiar journals published in the county. The Fort Henderson *Meddler*, issued only semi-occasionally, was the work of two young lawyers, their personality long unknown, who stirred up the community with accounts of all the gossip and scandals going. Very yellow copies of this journal are still in existence. In the same year, J. Taylor Bradt published in Horseheads a newspaper which he called the Chemung County *Patriot and Central Advocate*. It was established to advocate the making of Horseheads the county seat of the new county that was contemplated. The project failed, but if the smart town did not become the geographical capital it has become the political capital of the county, all the conventions of all the parties being always held there. A boys' amateur weekly, called *The Young American*, the first effort of the kind in this country, if not in the world, was published in Elmira during this period. The first daily published in the county was in 1847. It was called *The Karlon*, and was published by literary characters of considerable distinction of the time, the Rev. C. C. Burr, his wife Celia Burr, and "my brother Heman." It had "telegraphic news," as the telegraph came into the county, the first line built from Ithaca, even before the railroad arrived. The newspaper did not last long, less than a year.

Closing the period.—Just as the period of which we are writing was closing, as though to make the past more misty, dim, and unreal, and the future promise to be brighter and lighter, illuminating gas was introduced into the county at Elmira. A company formed in Albany, N. Y., built the works in 1849, and in the spring of 1850 the business was in full operation.

PART III

Military Affairs in the County

And there was mounting in hot haste: the steed,
The mustering squadron, and the clattering car
Went pouring forward with impetuous speed,
  And swiftly forming in the ranks of war;
  And the deep thunder peal on peal afar;
And near, the beat of the alarming drum
  Roused up the soldier.—CHILDE HAROLD.

  Their armor rings on a fairer field
    Than Greek or Roman ever trod,
  For Freedom's sword is the blade they wield,
    And the light above them the smile of God.
                  —PROCTOR.

The County During the War.

Military organizations. — The Chemung valley always possessed much military spirit, as was naturally to be expected of a locality whose history begins with a battle. In the old days there were no uniformed companies, but men capable of bearing arms met at certain stated times during the year, furnishing their own accoutrements, were drilled a little, marched a little, maneuvred their guns, and then it all ended with a general jollification. The traditions of these occasions, and in a few instances, the memories of these "general training days," as they were called, bring up scenes of great merriment and amusement. In a few individual cases representatives of the valley were connected with the War of 1812 with England. About 1834, a regular company was organized; largely through the efforts and activity of General W. R. Judson.[60] It made its first public parade in 1840

[60]General JUDSON was very active in other than the military affairs of the county. He was a saddler and harness-maker by trade, having been an apprentice of Cooley & Maxwell. He came to the valley when a lad, from Otsego County, N. Y., in 1812. He was in business for many years in Elmira. In the State of Kansas in 1856 he bought a large tract of land and founded a town thereupon, which he named Elmira. He was an exceedingly enthusiastic politician, and held many offices, county, State, and national. He became the Colonel of the militia regiment assigned to that portion of the State in which the county was located. He was the commanding officer of a Kansas Regiment of Cavalry during the war, and served with dis-

at the funeral of Col. John Hendy.[61] It was called
"The Elmira Guards," and continued in more or
less active existence nearly twenty years, being
succeeded in 1858 by "The Southern Tier Rifles,"
an organization that is still referred to with considerable pride. Under the command of Capt.
Henry C. Hoffman, it was most perfectly disciplined,
and one of the "crack" companies of the State.

When President Lincoln, on April 15, 1861, issued
his first call for troops, the appeal reached Elmira
on the afternoon of that day. A public meeting
was called for the same evening. It was tumul-
tuously attended. Most of the members of the
"Southern Tier Rifles" volunteered at once, and
the company under the command of Capt. Nat. B.
Fowler, became Company K of the Twenty-third
N. Y. Volunteers. It was largely a local regiment, and the first one organized in the county.
It was mustered into the service of the United
States for two years, or unless sooner discharged,
on May 16, 1861, with 788 officers and men. Its
officers were: Colonel, Henry C. Hoffman;[62] lieuten-

tinction. He was wounded in an engagement at Fort
Smith, Ark.

[61]Among the members of this first company were N. W.
Gardiner, a hatter; Joseph Hoffman, a saddler; Henry
Voorhees, a carpenter; Henry Hill, a merchant; R. B.
Sharpstein, an innkeeper; William Halliday, a merchant;
Wakeman Merwin, a saddler and harnessmaker, and Charles
Orwan, a gunsmith.

[62]Colonel HOFFMAN was one of the many active, energetic,
and enterprising business men of whose nativity within its
borders Chemung County has good reason to be proud.
His father was WILLIAM HOFFMAN, a sturdy, long-headed
man of German descent, who took up a large tract of land
to the west of Elmira late in the 18th century. He had a
number of sons who inherited his sterling qualities, and added

ant-colonel, Nirom M. Crane; major; William M. Gregg; adjutant, William W. Hayt; quartermaster, Myron H. Mandeville; surgeon, Seymour Churchill; assistant surgeon, William A. Medill; sergeant-major, Archibald N. Devoe; quartermaster-sergeant, Hiram T. Smith; drum-major, Miles Terrill; fife-major, Julius C. Smead.

The Twenty-third was a faithful, highly popular organization, and made an honorable record during its term of service. It was mustered out on May 23, 1863.

On July 30, 1861, Elmira was made one of the three military depots of the State, and a military rendezvous by the general government.[63] Officers of the regular army were sent there on duty.[64]

In 1863 Elmira was made the headquarters of the district as well as for the western division of the State, comprising the last eleven congressional districts thereof, for the reception of volunteers and drafted men. It was placed in the command of Gen. A. S. Diven.

greatly to the business, social, agricultural, and political importance of the county. COLONEL HOFFMAN was a member of the Board of Supervisors of the county three times, representing the town of Horseheads and was twice a Member of Assembly for the county.

[63]On the part of the State, the commanding officer of the post was Gen. R. B. Van Valkenburg, of Bath. He was succeeded by Colonel Eastman, of the United States Army, and he by Gen. Benjamin F. Tracy, of the Volunteers.

[64]The mustering and disbursing officers of the post of the regular army were Gen. W. W. Averill, a West Point graduate, who received his early education at the Elmira Academy. He became a distinguished cavalry officer during the war. He was succeeded by Capt. J. I. Tidball, Major Arthur T. Lee, Captain La Rhett L. Livingstone, and Capt. J. Riley Reid.

The number of military organizations.—From April 1861, to April 1865, there were twenty-four organizations belonging to the infantry arm of the service mustered in at Elmira, numbering 18,171 officers and men. To these are to be added four artillery organizations, with 973 officers and men; and six cavalry organizations with 1,650 officers and men, making a total of 20,796 soldiers forwarded from Elmira during the war. There were a number of individual instances of men entering the service not attached to organizations raised or mustered in at Elmira, which would raise the total forwarded from that city in round numbers to at least 25,000.

A complete company was raised in Horseheads and was assigned to the Thirty-eighth N. Y. V., as Company I.[65] It was mustered in on June 8, 1861. Almost every member came from the town of Horseheads. Its captain was Calvin S. Dewitt, a former member of the Twenty-third Regiment. It was in the first battle of Bull Run.

The Fiftieth Engineers.—Particular interest centered about the Fiftieth Engineers, as it was, officers and men alike, largely made up of citizens of the county and near neighborhood. It was mustered into service on September 18, 1861, as "Stuart's Independent Volunteers," taking its name from Gen. Charles B. Stuart, of Geneva, N. Y. Companies E and G were largely recruited in Millport and vicinity. Their respective captains were: Ira

---

[65]A curious, although perhaps not unusual, incident is connected with the annals of this company. First Sergeant William E. Straight was reported dead, and funeral services were held in his honor in Elmira. After some time he returned home, having been wounded and taken prisoner.

L. Spaulding, and W. W. Personius. The captain
of Company "H" was Gen. Edmund O. Beers.⁶⁶

The Eighty-sixth Regiment.—In the Eighty-sixth
regiment, called "The Steuben Rangers," was one
company so full of Chemung County men that it
deserved to be called a "home company." It was
Company E, of which Thomas F. Shoemaker was
captain. His first lieutenant was John Gilbert
Copley, who afterwards became the county clerk
of Chemung County. In Company F Capt. Henry
G. Harrower, of Big Flats, was the commanding
officer.

The surgeon of the Eighty-ninth Regiment was
Dr. Truman Hoffman Squire.⁶⁷

Capt. William M. Crosby was a teacher in a commercial college in Elmira. He recruited a company

⁶⁶GENERAL BEERS was the son of Jabez Beers, a carpenter,
who came to Elmira from Orange County, N. Y., in 1827.
He was one of thirteen children. He was a member of the
old "Elmira Guards" in 1847 and until that company disbanded in 1854. In 1857 he joined "The Southern Tier
Rifles." In the Fiftieth Engineers he rose to the rank of
Lieutenant-Colonel. After the war he continued his services in various positions in the State militia, and was made
Brigadier-General of the State forces located in the district
in which the county is situated. He was an active and
successful politician and served one term as Sheriff of the
county. He won the respect, confidence, and even the love
of his fellow-citizens, by a life of kind-heartedness, probity
and perfect honesty.

⁶⁷DR. SQUIRE was one of the most eminent surgeons of the
county and State. He came to Elmira from Herkimer
County, N. Y., in 1849. He was promoted to be Division
Field Surgeon under General Burnside, and the Surgeon-
General of the Army reported of him that he considered him
one of the most efficient surgeons in the Army of the Potomac.
He wrote admirably on medical subjects for home and for-
eign publications, and was a member of societies in this
country and abroad.

all from that city, and composed largely of young men in attendance upon his school. It was mustered into service as Company K of the 103d N. Y. V.

The favorite of all.—The favorite organization of all, however, would seem to have been the 107th Regiment. It was very quickly recruited, equipped, and forwarded to the front. The regimental feeling is, even now, very strong, and annual meetings are held on September 17, the anniversary of the battle of Antietam, where the regiment suffered severely. The county owes its only monumental remembrance of the war to the statue, the figure of a soldier in marble and granite, standing in the court-house park on Lake Street, in Elmira, which was unveiled on September 17, 1882. Many of the old Twenty-third joined the ranks of the 107th as officers and men. It was mustered into the service on August 13, 1862, with 1,016 members. Its officers were: Colonel, Robert B. Van Valkenburgh; lieutenant-colonel, Alexander S. Diven;[68] major,

---

[68]GENERAL DIVEN was, in many ways, one of the most distinguished men, if not the most distinguished man, of his day in the county. He was the son of John Diven, who came into the county from Pennsylvania in 1790. General Diven came to Elmira in 1845 as a member of a firm of lawyers that became widely known, Diven, Hathaway & Woods. He was an intensely public-spirited man, being largely interested in the building of the Erie Railroad, the Elmira and Williamsport Railroad, and in a great many other local enterprises of magnitude and of value and interest to the county. He was a State Senator and a Member of Congress, where he took high rank as an orator and business man. General Diven died in 1905. His eldest son, George M. Diven, the dean at present of the Chemung County bar in actual practice, was equally public-spirited, and conducted successfully a number of local enterprises of large importance. He was for many years the President of the Elmira Board of Education.

Gabriel L. Smith; adjutant, Hull Fanton; quartermaster, Edward P. Graves; surgeon, Patrick H. Flood;[69] assistant surgeon, James D. Hewitt; Chaplain, Ezra F. Crane; sergeant-major, John R. Lindsay; quartermaster-sergeant, Lucien B. Chidsey; commissary sergeant, Henry Inscho; hospital steward, John M. Thro.

The captain of Company B of this regiment was Lathrop Baldwin, Jr.[70]

The regiment made a very brilliant record, participating in some of the bloodiest and most decisive engagements of the war. It was with General Sherman on his "March to the Sea," and was mustered out of service on June 5, 1865.

---

[69]DR. FLOOD was another popular and successful physician of Elmira. He came originally from Northampton County, Pa., and to Elmira in 1852, at once taking a high position in his profession. He was an active and ambitious politician, served two terms as Mayor of the City of Elmira, and was a member of all the local medical societies. He was the Surgeon of the First Division, Twentieth Army Corps, at the close of the war. His son, Thomas S. Flood, has been Alderman and Mayor of the City of Elmira, and Member of Congress, and his youngest son, Henry, was postmaster of the city of Elmira.

[70]CAPTAIN BALDWIN was a member of the Baldwin family that came early into the valley. He was slender and delicate of figure, with the gentlest of dispositions, but with a spirit and force of character that was characteristic of his family, and he made a good soldier. He was a son of a soldier of the War of 1812, and grandson of a soldier of the Revolution. His father was deputy sheriff of the county, and was the first occupant of the new County Court House in 1824. Captain Baldwin was a printer and a newspaper man. He was promoted to be Major soon after the One Hundred and Seventh reached the field. At the fierce battle of Peach Tree Creek, Ga., on June 22, 1864, he was mortally wounded, and died the following month. His commission as Lieutenant-Colonel, to which office he had been promoted, is dated on the day of the battle. The first post of the Grand Army of the Republic, and one of the first organized of the country, bears his name.

The 141st.—The 141st Regiment was also entitled
to be called a "home regiment," as it had three
full companies raised in the county. It followed
very quickly in the wake of the 107th, being mustered into the service a month later, in September,
1862, with 956 officers and men. The two reg-
ments rivalled each other in local popularity. The
officers of the 141st were: Colonel, Samuel G. Hathaway;[71] lieutenant-colonel, James C. Beecher; major,
John W. Dinniny; adjutant, Henry L. Pierson;
quartermaster, Silas Haight; surgeon, John W.
Robinson; assistant surgeon, Orlando S. Greenman; chaplain, Thomas K. Beecher; sergeant-
major, L. A. Hazard; quartermaster-sergeant, Miles
W. Hanley; hospital steward, Harris Sawyer; principal musician, George Gray.[72]

[71]COLONEL HATHAWAY was an exceptional man in physical
appearance and mental capacity, an unusually fine speaker
and brilliant lawyer. He came to Elmira in 1835, from
Cortland County, N. Y., and was in partnership first with
Judge James Dunn, and afterward with Judge Hiram Gray.
He is best remembered, however, as a member of the famous
firm of Diven, Hathaway & Woods. He was a close political and personal friend of John Van Buren, son of President
Martin Van Buren. He died in 1864, while in service.

[72]Adjutant Pierson was succeeded as soon as the regiment
went into the field, by Robert M. McDowell, a grandson of
Capt. Daniel McDowell, one of the earliest settlers in the
valley. He made a military record for himself quite in keeping with the family name, which is such a distinguished one
in the history of the county. He was educated as a civil
engineer, and during the war was chief topographical engineer on the staff of Gen. Joseph Hooker. For many years,
as mining engineer, he was connected with an extensive
system of railroads in the West.
The Lieutenant-Colonel and Chaplain of the regiment
were both clergymen, sons of Lyman Beecher and brothers
of Henry Ward Beecher. The Sergeant-Major, L. A. Hazard,
was a newspaper man, exceedingly bright and amiable, long
connected with the Elmira *Gazette*, and at one time part

Company C of the regiment was commanded by
Elisha G. Baldwin.[13]   Company K by Capt. Wilbur
F. Tuttle; of Big Flats. The regiment was mus-
tered out on June 8, 1865.

The 161st.—In this regiment one whole company
was recruited from Chemung County, and scattered
all through its ranks were Chemung County men.
The company mentioned was C, and was raised
and commanded by Capt. R. R. R. Dumars.[14]   The
regiment saw nearly all its service; and it was very
rough, in the campaigns around New Orleans. It
participated in the capture of Port Hudson; and
was the first regiment to enter Mobile after the sur-
render of that city. It was mustered out of service
on September 20, 1865.

The 179th.—This was the last regiment entirely
or partially made up from the county, that was
raised in Elmira. It contained many members

proprietor thereof, with his younger brother Charles Hazard.
A post of the Grand Army of the Republic in Elmira is
named in his honor and memory. Dr. O. S. Greenman
surgeon of the regiment, was a successful and highly-regarded
physician of Horseheads.

[13]CAPTAIN BALDWIN was another member of that numerous
family of Baldwins that was so prominent in all the affairs
of the county from its very first settlement. He was a
printer and newspaper man. At the bloody battle of Peach
Tree Creek, Ga., both his regiment and the One Hundred
and Seventh suffered terribly. He was in command of his
regiment and it stood its ground nobly. For gallant services
there he was promoted to be Major.

[14]CAPTAIN DUMARS was a printer and newspaper man, and
in such connection was always popular and prominent. He
established the Elmira *Daily Press*, and afterward became
a leading spirit on the *Advertiser*. He served one term as
Alderman from his ward in the Common Council of the City
of Elmira. His first lieutenant was Orlando N. Smith, a
most estimable man, a son of Dr. Norman Smith, the first

who had belonged to the old "Twenty-third," and
who had in the brief period earned the title of
"veterans." It was mustered into service during
the month of September; 1864; with 846 officers
and men. It was commanded by Col. William M.
Gregg.[15] The regiment retained and increased the
reputation for daring and bravery that had been
fairly earned by the earlier local organizations, and
the story of its services will be recited hereafter
with pride by the descendants of those who were
in its ranks. At the assault on Petersburg, Va.,
on April 2, 1865, the regiment suffered terribly.
For gallant conduct there, Colonel Gregg was bre-
veted brigadier-general. The regiment was mustered out of service on June 8; 1865. For the brief
period it was in the field there was crowded into
the time a service of hardship and danger that some
organizations did not experience during the whole
war

In March and April, 1865, the last regimental
organization was begun in Elmira, and seven companies were mustered in with 584 officers and men.
Its services were never required, and its organization was never completed.

Artillery.—In the artillery arm of the service,

dentist to settle in Elmira, coming there in 1835. Orlando
Smith was largely interested in the Elmira Fire Department.

[15]COLONEL GREGG was a descendant of John Gregg, who
came into the valley in the late years of the 18th century. He
was a saddler and harnessmaker, and was always interested
in the military and political affairs of the county. He was
one of the three railroad mail agents first appointed, in 1849,
to run on the Erie Railroad, their route being between
Elmira and Binghamton. He served one term as Sheriff
of the county. A post of the Grand Army of the Republic
in Horseheads is named in his honor.

there were four organizations; regiments, and bat-
teries mustered in at Elmira during the war, and
although some men of the county were members
thereof, none of the companies could be called local
organizations.

The Cavalry.—In the cavalry arm of the service
there were six organizations mustered in at Elmira.
They had a number of representatives from the
county; although relatively very small compared
with the infantry.

Tenth Regiment.—One of these was the 10th Regiment of Mounted Volunteers. It was a very popular organization in the county. It was mustered
in on December; 1861, with 991 officers and men.
Its commanding officer was Col. William Irvine.[16]
One of the lieutenants of the regiment was Luther
L. Barney,[17] who had been very active in the organization of his company.

The Twenty-fourth New York Cavalry had one
company; that of Capt. L. L. Doolittle, which had
a number of Chemung County men on its rolls.

The Seventeenth New York Cavalry, afterwards
consolidated with the First Veteran Cavalry, had
two companies, almost exclusively composed of
Chemung County men. It was mustered into serv-

---

[16]COLONEL IRVINE was a busy and enterprising politician.
He was at one time the Adjutant-General of the State.
Subsequently he removed to California, where he became
a successful business man and lawyer.

[17]LIEUTENANT BARNEY made a useful and competent officer.
He rose to the rank of Captain and served as Assistant Adjutant-General on the division staff of General Gregg. After
the war he engaged in the insurance business, and attained
most responsible positions with some of the strongest companies in the country.

ice on July 30, 1863. Two captains in this regiment, William L. Morgan, and John Whitley, Jr., personally enlisted, with two exceptions, every man on their rolls.[78]

The lack of silver change.—There was one deprivation in these times that caused very serious annoyance and inconvenience—the entire and complete disappearance of silver change. There had been no quarters, dimes, or nickels at that time, and the pennies or cents were great copper discs that no one but children hankered after. The whole country had depended on Mexican or Spanish coinage called "pillared" pieces, by reason of the peculiar design on one face. They were called two shillings, shillings, and sixpences. It may not be recollected that our present serviceable American decimal coinage was not adopted until after the war. Postage stamps were used until they became soiled, sticky, and obliterated, and individual dealers[79] got out fractional currency in vari-

[78]Captain Morgan had resigned from the One Hundred and Seventh to raise his company. He was killed in Virginia in an engagement with Mosby's men. Captain Whitley was a newspaper man, and was part proprietor of the Elmira *Daily Press.* The first lieutenant of Captain Morgan's company, E. V. Coulton, was one of the early schoolmasters of the county. He was long remembered as a severe physical disciplinarian with the switch and strap, an exercise that fully prepared him for good service as a cavalry officer. Sam A. Paine, who had already seen service in the One Hundred and Third Infantry, was a member of this company. Since the war he has made an enviable reputation for himself as a crisp, ready, bright newspaper writer.

[79]One shrewd financier had printed five-cent shinplasters that were payable when presented in sums amounting to five dollars. He issued ninety-nine of these little bills. It was finance of a new character, but it worked.

ous amounts less than a dollar. The city of Elmira finally issued neatly engraved bills in denominations less than a dollar,[80] and they were used until the Government printed the convenient postal fractional currency in 1863.

Gateway between the North and South.—The location of the county of Chemung is peculiar. It has been called, and with considerable reason, the "gateway between the North and South." From time immemorial the aborigines used the Chemung Valley[81] in going on the warpath or on missions of peace from Canada and the northwestern part of the State to the South, and what are now the States of Virginia and North and South Carolina. It was the route that in those unhappy days runaway blacks took to escape from bondage and reach places of freedom. Elmira became quite a noted station of the "under-ground railroad," where the unfortunates always found rest, recuperation, and assistance on their journey.

It was because of its situation that the valley was chosen, first for a military rendezvous and then for the location of a military prison. It was easy of access from either way, both North and South.

---

[80]The idea was conceived and put into practice by S. C. Reynolds, the President, and F. C. Steele, the Treasurer of the Board of Trustees of the village of Elmira. They received much commendation from the citizens and business men of the county for their action, and the artistic character of the bills. A very few of these bills are still in existence and are held of abnormal value.

[81]A look at the map will demonstrate this clearly. The route between Canada and Fort Niagara or Buffalo leads down the Genessee Valley to the upper waters of a tributary of the Chemung, thence down that river to the Susquehanna, and by that stream to Maryland and Virginia.

Troops could be forwarded from there very rapidly, with the least delay, and it could be defended with little effort from the approach of any enemy.

Prison Camp.—"The Rebel Prison Camp," as it was called, for the care of prisoners taken in war was established in May, 1864. It forms an incident; the most important happening in the county since the battle of Newtown, with which the history of the valley begins, and it is of more than local interest. Every step was taken to insure the comfort and the safety of the prisoners. The situation chosen was in one of the loveliest and most fruitful portions of the valley, just to the west of the village of Elmira. It was about thirty acres in extent, and lay adjoining the river with a small lake or pond of living water within its boundaries. It was surrounded by a close board fence twelve feet in height, on the exterior of which, within four or five feet from the top, ran a wooden pathway, along which guards constantly paced night and day.

At first ordinary "A" tents were provided for the prisoners, but before the winter set in barracks were built of boards; in which the men were comfortably housed. Abundant provision was made for the supply of food.

The first detachment of prisoners arrived in the latter part of June, 1864, and the whole number cared for from this time to August, 1865, when the camp was broken up; was 11,916 men; a large proportion of them coming from North Carolina.

The prison guard.—The prison was guarded at first by two infantry regiments of the regular army and a battery of the Fourth United States Artillery,

afterwards by two regiments of the "Invalid Corps."
The name of this organization was subsequently
changed to the "Veteran Reserve Corps."

There were few attempts at escape among the
prisoners; and only one or two successful ones.[82]

An attractive place.—The camp, while in existence, was the most attractive spot in the valley,
and was daily visited by hundreds from all over
the country. Along the street that formed one of
its boundaries was erected a long row of booths,
where were displayed a variety of articles of food
and drink to attract the attention and desire of
the sightseer. It was like a perennial fair.

The prisoners occupied themselves in such ways
as suited their tastes or inclinations. Some attended to the lawns and gardens, by which the spot
was beautified, and for which they received pay;
others cut ornaments from wood or constructed
them from horsehair, bits of coal or other materials.[83]

The food provided was plentiful and of the best
quality. During the existence of the camp; only

[82]One of these escaped by passing out of the main gate
as a son of one of the officers in charge of the camp, whom
he strongly resembled. Another one allowed himself to be
nailed up in a coffin and passed out of the camp in the dead
wagon.

[83]Col. Samuel B. Hayman, a grandnephew of "Mad
Anthony Wayne" of revolutionary times, was the Comman-
dant of the Post during the latter part of the war, and made
frequent visits to the camp, He owned, and he was very
proud of it, a white horse, remarkable for its beauty and
the plentifulness of its mane and tail. He took the animal
to the camp once. He hitched it to a post and went into
the officer's quarters on business, or for social pleasure, and
was gone some time. When he returned his horse was there,
but it possessed no mane or tail. Very soon thereafter
appeared some very tasteful ornaments for sale, all made
of white horsehair!

a little over a year, there were issued to and con-
sumed by the prisoners, 13,000 barrels of flour, and
of meat, salt and fresh, nearly 2,000,000 pounds!
There were savings from the rations allowed by
the Government that were turned into cash and
went to the benefit of the prisoners themselves,
making what was called a "prison fund." When
the camp was broken up there remained in the
bank to the credit of this fund, $92,000!

There was much sickness in the camp, many of
the prisoners arriving in a desperate physical con-
dition, and at one time the smallpox broke out,
from which there were many fatalities. There
were 2,994 cases of death during the existence of
the camp. Of these, 2,988 were buried at Woodlawn, the city's cemetery; three were buried on
the bank of the river, but were washed away by
the great flood of 1865, and three were buried down
the river in the neighborhood of the pesthouse.

An accurate record was kept of those buried at
Woodlawn, and there are many pathetic incidents
related of persons from the South seeking sons or
brothers or husbands lost in the war, and finding
their bodies carefully and tenderly laid away there.

The hospital accommodations were of the first
class, with all the appliances of surgery and medicine known at the time. They were in charge, in
the beginning, of Dr. William C. Wey.[84]

---

[84]DR. WEY was one of the most distinguished physicians
of the State. He came to Elmira in 1849. He was connected
by marriage with the Covell family, who helped so much in
the earliest times to make the history of Chemung County.
In 1871 he was the President of the State Medical Society,
and served in that position with great distinction. He was

The Sanitary Fair Conflagration.—An incident
connected with this period, somewhat resulting
from the war as one of its disasters, creating great
distress all through the county, was the burning, in
March, 1864, of the First Presbyterian Church. As
was the custom of the time, a fair to raise funds
for the Sanitary Commission, an organization formed
for the benefit and comfort of the soldiers at the front,
had been arranged; and it was held in the church,
which was in the course of construction. The bare
beams and timbers were profusely decorated with
evergreens. In lighting the gas one evening a
burning match touched these inflammable ornaments, and in five minutes the whole interior was
in flames. It was at "tea time," and there were
few persons in the building. Two were burned to
death, Maxey Manning Converse,[85] and Frederick
Hart, a son of William E. Hart. The loss other-
wise was incalculable, as many valuable exhibits,
oil-paintings, old furniture, and tableware, tapes-
try, and other articles had been loaned for purposes
of decoration or sale.

The one riot.—One riot, not very successful or
destructive, marked this period in the history of
the county, and excited very lively apprehensions
in the minds of the citizens. Members of a Michi-
gan regiment, on their way home to be mustered
out, in the exuberance of their feelings became

prominently connected with the affairs of the Elmira Reformatory. He died on June 30, 1897.

[85]MR. CONVERSE was an accomplished musician, a member
of a very ancient family, and came to Elmira from Connecticut. His son, Charles Cozart Converse, has achieved great
distinction in the musical, literary, and business world.

very lively, tipped over loads of hay in the streets of Elmira, tore down signs and awnings, and behaved in a way that could hardly be called playful. They got away beyond the patrol guard, but when a regiment from the prison camp came trotting down to quell the tumult, the disturbance and trouble didn't last very long after its appearance. An entirely innocent man leaning on a big wheel of a wagon, was the only victim. A shot was fired from some unknown quarter; and it took effect upon him. He dropped dead where he stood. No one received any punishment for the occurrence.

PART IV

Chemung County during the latter half of the XIX with glimpses of the XX Century

---

The Times are the masquerade of the Eternities: trivial to the dull, tokens of noble and majestic agents to the wise; the receptacle in which the past leaves its history; the quarry out of which the genius of to-day is building up the Future. We talk of the world, but we mean a few men and women. If you speak of the age you mean your own platoon of people.

—EMERSON.

The Latter Half of the XIXth,

WITH GLIMPSES OF THE OPENING OF THE XXTH
CENTURY.

The period comprising the latter half of the 19th century was of great interest to the county and valley. There was a constant increase in everything that makes life interesting and valuable.

Perhaps the most important was the means of getting about and the completer connection with the outside world. Facilities for this purpose were added constantly to those already possessed by the county.

New facilities for doing business.—On January 1, 1853, work was begun on a railroad to connect Elmira with Williamsport, Pa.; a distance of about seventy miles south, and on August 1, 1854, it was completed and in operation. In 1863 and 1866 this line with one from Elmira to Canandaigua came, by long leases, under the control of the Pennsylvania Railroad Company, and was operated by the Northern Central Railroad Company.

In 1876 two lines of road were completed, one originally called the Utica, Ithaca, and Elmira Railroad; its aim being to reach the coal fields of Blossburg, Pa. This road was largely due to the business sagacity of Joseph Rodbourn, and Ulysses and William K. Breese, backed by the money and influence of Ezra Cornell. The line

ran over the hills from Elmira to Ithaca.[86]   It became, in time, the Elmira, Cortland and Northern
Railroad, its northern terminus being at Canastota,
and afterward was a branch of the Lehigh Valley
Railroad.

The other road was called the Elmira and State
Line Railroad, and ran southwesterly from Elmira
to Blossburg, Pa., reaching the Pennsylvania coal
fields there.   It subsequently, in 1882, came under
the control of the Erie road, and is known as the
"Tioga branch" thereof.

In 1870 the Lehigh Valley Railroad was extended
to Elmira,[87] using a third rail from Waverly, on the
Erie road.   This led to the change of the Erie broad
guage track to the "standard" gauge, the work
being completed in 1883.

Another trunk-line, the Delaware, Lackawanna
and Western, reached Elmira in 1882, its first pas-
senger-train running into the station at that city
on April 3 of that year.

Other geographical divisions.—A number of new

---

[86]Joseph Rodbourn was a very unique and industrious
citizen of Breesport, in the town of Horseheads, through
which hamlet the road ran.   He came there about 1850.
His hands were always full of undertakings that were for
the benefit of the village and the neighborhood where he
had taken up his residence.   For many years he was the
County Overseer of the Poor, the county buildings having been
located in Breesport in 1836.   In Breesport he built a grist-
mill and sawmill, both of very large capacity, and made the
village hum with the bustle of industry and business.   The
shops of the new railroad were located in Breesport.   A
post-office was established there on November 19, 1853.
Mr. Rodbourn was the first postmaster.

[87]At that time, and for some years afterward, the Lehigh
Valley Road ran over the tracks of the Erie from Sayre, Pa.,
to Buffalo.

townships were formed in the county during this period. Horseheads was taken from Elmira Township and formed into one by itself on February 7; 1854.[88]

On April 17; 1854; Chemung County was about cut in two. Its northern portion, being the towns of Catherine; Dix, and a little of Cayuta, were sliced away to help make the new county of Schuyler. There was much feeling aroused by this action of the Legislature. Chemung was a snug; compact little county as it was; reaching from the lake to the Pennsylvania line, and all portions of it were bound together by ties of memory; tradition; and interest that should have kept it together; as it was originally formed in 1788, when Chemung Township was organized.[89]

On the same date part of the old township of Cayuta was saved to Chemung, and with a portion of Erin Township was made into the township of Van Etten.[90]

Once more; on April 7, 1856, the northern part

---

[88]The first town-meeting was held on February 14, 1854, and Samuel H. Maxwell was elected Supervisor. He served three terms in that capacity, and in his third term he was chosen Chairman of the Board.

[89]The new county did not fall into ways of pleasantness and peace. For thirteen years there was a quarrel there as to the location of the county seat. On the side of one of these contentions was the Hon. Jeremiah McGuire. He was an Irish lad, born in Dublin. In 1849 he settled in the village of Havana, then in Chemung County. In 1873 he was the Member of Assembly from Schuyler County, and the same year removed to Elmira. In 1874 he was the Member of Assembly from Chemung County, and served as the Speaker of that body. He died in 1889.

[90]The first town meeting was held on May 9, 1854, and George B. Hall was chosen Supervisor.

of the township of Chemung was taken and there
was formed from it the township of Baldwin.[91]

But the most important change of the period
affected the city of Elmira. On April 7, 1864, it
was made into a city of five wards.[92] In 1872, the
city was again divided into seven wards, and in
1899 it became a city of twelve wards.

There was one more change in the civil divisions
and the last one so far. The township of Ashland,
named in honor of the home of Henry Clay, was
erected on April 21, 1867, to form which portions
of the townships of Elmira and Southport were
taken.[93]

Educational Institutions.—Quite in keeping with
pretty much all the other portions of this country
the matter of the education of the children engaged
the attention of the citizens, and the interest therein
far from abating, never once ceased to grow and
increase.[94]

---

[91]The first town-meeting was held on May 6, 1856, and
William H. Little was chosen Supervisor.

[92]The first Common Council met on April 19, 1864. John
I. Nicks was the last President of the Board of Trustees of
the village of Elmira. John Arnot, Jr., was the first Mayor
of the City of Elmira.

[93]The first town-meeting in Ashland was held on May 4,
1867. Richard C. Lockwood was chosen Supervisor.

The term of office in the Board of Supervisors of the
county show some remarkable records. George W. Buck
served fifteen years as member of the Board from Chemung
Township, and was Chairman of the Board six years. Jesse
L. Cooley served as Clerk of the Board for ten years.

[94]In SOUTHPORT there are sixteen school districts and
fourteen school-houses, most of them organized and built
during the period of which we write. In CHEMUNG there
are seventeen school districts. In HORSEHEADS the first
school-house was built in 1800. In 1850 a school of high
grade was opened, Ezra Roberts being the first principal.

In Elmira there had been two district school-houses, an academy, and a number of private schools. The academy was a large building situated on Baldwin Street. It was first used as the Presbyterian Church, built about 1821, and was removed to the lot it occupied in 1836.[95]

In 1859 the Legislature of the State provided for a Board of Education to have charge of the

He subsequently removed to Elmira where he established and conducted a private school of considerable reputation. In 1865 a school was organized in Horseheads as a Union Free School, being in advance of the general law for free schools. The first principal under this new system was Sylvester D. Boorom. A Board of Education is in charge of this institution, and the school has grown to large and influential proportions. In BIG FLATS there are eight districts and the same number of school-houses. In the village of the name, there have been three school-houses, one built in 1815, the red school-house built in 1837, and the one now in use, built in 1853. In ERIN there were, in 1833, three school-houses, and the interest therein has not abated. In VAN ETTEN the first school was taught by Mrs. Jonathan Baker, in 1803. There are now twelve school districts in the township. In Van Ettenville, in this township, there was organized a Union School in 1882, which is in charge of a Board of Education. The institution flourished from the start, and it is one of the most popular and favorite public interests of the town. In BALDWIN a school-house was built at "Hammond's Corners" in 1852. In CATLIN the first school-house was built in 1820. There are now in the township eleven school-houses and parts of three districts.

[95]These district schools were in charge, at one time or another of men who became distinguished afterwards in the various walks of life. Among them may be named Gen. A. S. Diven, Judge Ariel Thurston and Hugh Riddle, who attained great distinction in the railroad business, being at one time President of the Rock Island Railroad Company; and at the Academy were graduated those who achieved prominent places in the world. Among these are the Hon. Charles B. Farwell, at one time United States Senator from Illinois; Rear-Admiral Francis A. Roe, United States Navy; Major-General William W. Averill, U. S. A., General Hull Fanton, and Francis Collingood, a civil engineer of renown.

public schools of the town. There were five districts erected at first, and a primary school connected with district No. 1.[96] There are now twelve
districts.

The First Free Academy was completed in 1862.
In 1891 preparations were begun for the erection
of a new building, and it was completed and occupied in 1893.

The Elmira College for women.—This institution
the first one in the country chartered to bestow
upon women similar degrees to those granted to
young men, was authorized on April 13, 1855, its
name at that time being changed from the "Elmira
Collegiate Seminary" to the "Elmira Female College." It was opened in October, 1853. In 1890
a music hall was added in connection with the
institution, costing $10,000; by the munificence
of Solomon L. Gillett, a wealthy merchant of Elmira.[97]

Religious Advantages.—There is hardly a spot

---

[96]The first meeting of the Board of Education was held
on April 19, 1859. The commissioners were: Erastus L. Hart,
John Arnot, Orrin Robertson, Elijah N. Barbour, Ariel S.
Thurston, Stephen McDonald, Archibald Robertson, Civilian
Brown, and Shubael B. Denton. The first President of the
Board was Erastus L. Hart, and the first secretary and
superintendent, S. R. Scofield.

[97]The institution was greatly indebted in its inception to
Simeon Benjamin, who gave very liberally for its foundation.
The Rev Dr. A. W. Cowles was its first president, and continued to act as such for thirty-six years. Many eminent
teachers have been connected with the institution. Its
semi-centennial was celebrated in 1905 with great display
and much enthusiasm. At Christmas, 1906, Dr. Cowles was
made President emeritus of the college, and a pension of
$1,200 a year was bestowed upon him from the Carnegie
fund, for eminence in the educational annals of the country.

in the whole county, however remote, that in some direction cannot be seen a steeple, pointing toward Heaven, indicating that there is a building there, where those of some denomination gather weekly and sometimes oftener for public worship.[98]

During this period Elmira had a great increase in the number of her churches. The First Presby-

[98]In BREESPORT, in the town of Horseheads, there are four churches, a Presbyterian church, built in 1875, a Methodist church, built in 1880, a Methodist Protestant Church, built in 1855, and a Baptist Church, built in 1856. In BIG FLATS the Methodist Church was built in 1868, a Presbyterian Church, built in 1829, and an Episcopal Church, built in 1867. In ASHLAND, at Wellsburg, there is a Baptist Church, built in 1812. It has a curious memory attached to it. The land on which the church stands and that adjoining, set off as a cemetery, was given to the Society by Henry Wells, for fifty cents! Also in Wellsburg the Methodist Church there was built in 1874. This society was organized in 1847, its first pastor being the Rev. Charles Davis. There is also in Wellsburg an Episcopal Church. In the township of BALDWIN at "Hammond's Corners" there is a building erected in 1852, that is used by seven different denominations. In HORSEHEADS a brick Baptist Church was dedicated on February 20, 1856. A Presbyterian Church, of which the Rev. C. C. Carr was pastor for twenty three years, was originally built in 1832. It was enlarged in 1859 and was still further enlarged and beautified in 1888. There is also in Horseheads an Episcopal Church, built in 1866-67. This society was organized on August 11, 1862. The Roman Catholic Church in Horseheads was built in 1866. An Elmira man, born and bred in that city, has been for some time the pastor of this church, Father William T. Dunn. The Methodist Church in Horseheads had its first class-meeting in 1827 in a new barn erected by Jonas Sayre. On November 25, 1834, the Society was incorporated as "First Society of the Methodist Episcopal Church in Horseheads." The first church building was erected in 1834. It was enlarged in 1856. In 1868 a parsonage was built. In this township a church or Society of Friends or Quakers was organized in 1860. In SOUTHPORT the First Baptist Church was built in 1853, the Society being regularly organized in May, 1855; a Methodist Church was also built in 1855, and the Presbyterian Church, built in 1839. In "Hendy Hollow," in this township, a Roman Catholic Church was built

terian Church provided the largest number
of changes. The "Independent Congregational
Church," which was the first to break away from
the old body, built its first church in 1851. The
present house of worship was built and occupied
in 1876. In June, 1854, the Rev. Thomas K.
Beecher⁹⁹ became the pastor of the church and
the name of the organization was changed to the
"Park Church." In 1860, what was at first known
as the Second Presbyterian Church of Elmira sepa-
rated from the old church. Its name subsequently
became the "Lake Street Presbyterian Church."
The church building was dedicated on June 13,
1862. In 1905 it was enlarged and improved.

---

in 1878. In CHEMUNG the Methodist Church was built in
1850, and a Baptist church, built in 1855 and dedicated on
February 3 of that year. In VAN ETTENVILLE a Baptist
Church was built in 1852 and a Methodist Church in 1883.
In SWARTWOOD, in the Township, a Hedding, Methodist
Church was built in 1826, and remodeled in 1883. In
VETERAN a Baptist Society, first organized and first known
as the "Free Religious Society," built a church in 1871.
In PINE VALLEY, in this township, a Methodist Church was
built and dedicated in November, 1889. Also in MILLPORT
a Methodist Church, originally built in 1833, was rebuilt
in 1867, and a Baptist Society organized in 1844, purchased
their church from the Presbyterians and rededicated it on
March 27, 1871, and St. Mark's Episcopal Church was consecrated here in January, 1888. In ERIN a Baptist Church
was built in 1874 and a Methodist Church in 1871. The
First Methodist Church is the only church in CATLIN. Its
cornerstone was laid on July 16, 1881, and it was dedicated
on March 8, 1882. In HORSEHEADS a colored church, called
the African Union Methodist Protestant Church was organized in 1860. In 1883 they built a brick church.

⁹⁹Mr. Beecher was probably the widest known of any
citizen of the county. He was a son of the famous Dr.
Lyman Beecher. He served as pastor of the church for
forty-six years and during his life was one of the most influential citizens of the county, his activity extending into
every field of endeavor. He died on March 14, 1900.

The Franklin Street Church was organized in 1882, the formal organization being perfected on January 17 of that year. The North Church, a further outgrowth from the old body, occupied its new church building in 1890.

Trinity Church rectory was finished and occupied in 1852, and the church building was opened for worship in July, 1858.[100] The Arnot Memorial Chapel, which is connected with Trinity Church, was consecrated in November, 1882, its corner-stone having been laid in 1880.

Grace Church, which is an offshoot of Trinity, was incorporated in 1864. The chapel it occupied for many years was erected in 1866. A new edifice was erected in 1904. St. Agnes Chapel, an off-spring of Grace Church, was dedicated on April 13, 1893.

The new Baptist Church was begun in the spring of 1889, and dedicated on May 15, 1892.[101] On May 6, 1854, some members of the church formed a new organization called at first the "Central Baptist Church," becoming however the "Madison Avenue Baptist Church." It remained in existence only a few years.

The "Hedding" Methodist Church was organized from the First Church on August 31, 1852. The "Centenary," another development of Methodism

---

[100]The Rev. William Paret, at one time rector of this church became the Bishop of Maryland. The Rev. George H. McKnight, who became rector of the church in 1869, served as such for thirty-six years. He died on March 15, 1905.

[101]The Rev. W. T. Henry came as pastor of this church in 1877, occupying the pulpit for the first time on March 27 of that year. He has served the church for almost thirty years.

was organized in 1872, and its church edifice was erected in 1884. Another church has recently been organized, and a church built on Maple Avenue.

There was a "Freewill Baptist Church" organized in 1869; and a church building erected by them in the same year. The first pastor was the Rev. Schuyler Aldrich.

A German Evangelical Church was organized on November 8, 1874, its pastor being the Rev. Mr. Loesch. Its church was subsequently located on Madison Avenue. The Roman Catholic Church has been prominent in Elmira and unusually active. The church of St. John the Baptist was organized in 1867. Its church building was built in 1891, and was consecrated on May 1; 1892. St. Patrick's is one of the most conspicuous churches in the city. It was built in 1871, and consecrated on December 13, 1875.[102] St. Mary's Catholic Church was first built in 1872, which was replaced in 1874. The church of St. Charles of Borromeo, located at Elmira Heights, was consecrated on November 2, 1904.

Those of the Hebrew faith have two places of worship. The congregation of B'nai Israel was organized in 1860, and their synagogue was built in 1863. The other congregation is called Shomer Hadoth.

There are also two churches for the colored people. The African Union Methodist Protestant

---

[102]This church is indebted to its pastor, the Rev. Father J. J. Bloomer, who to a Christian character adds a business tact and judgment that has made his career very successful both as a clergyman and man. He is much beloved by his people, and enjoys the confidence and respect of the whole community. He is the dean of the Elmira clergy, having served as pastor longer than any other minister now living.

Church was organized in 1850. Their first church building was erected in 1852, and the one built to replace it in 1879 and dedicated in August, 1880. An African Methodist Episcopal Zion Church grew out of this society in 1870. They built their church in 1871.

As closely allied to the work of the churches is the Young Men's Christian Association. A society of this name was organized in Elmira, the only one in the county, in July, 1858.[103] It occupied rooms for ten years, and in 1892 a building was erected for its use, and very recently another one was prepared for and occupied by it.

A Railway Young Men's Christian Association was organized in Elmira on May 12, 1878, and a well-equipped building was prepared for it in 1881.

Fraternal orders and associations. — Chemung County has been a rich field for the organization of secret orders for fraternal and charitable purposes.[104] Masonry in Elmira, in 1828, suffered an

---

[103]The first officers of this organization were: President, H. M. Partridge; vice-president, Seymour B. Fairman; recording secretary, Samuel R. Van Campen; corresponding secretary, A. R. Wright; treasurer, Socrates Ayres.

[104]All through the county there are organizations of goodly numbers, all showing much interest in the objects for which they were formed. In CHEMUNG Township Chemung Lodge No. 350, F. and A. M., was chartered on August 23, 1854, and Chemung Grange, No. 204, of the Patrons of Husbandry was organized in May, 1874. In HORSEHEADS a lodge of F. and A. M. named Horseheads Lodge, No. 364, was chart. ered, and held its first meeting on July 21, 1855. James A. Christie was designated as W. M. In 1862, the buildings the order occupied were burned, and the work of the lodge intermitted for two or three months. The Horseheads Chapter, No. 261, R. A. M., was instituted in April, 1871. The Chemung Valley Equitable Aid Union of Horseheads was organized in June, 1880. BIG FLATS has a lodge, No.

eclipse for fifteen years. In 1843, the old Union
Lodge No. 30 was resuscitated, and under the new
number, 90, again began its work. The Royal
Arch Chapter, No. 42, had been chartered on April
4, 1815. It, too, suffered an eclipse along with
Union Lodge, and in 1844 sprang again into life.
The Commandery of St. Omers, No. 19, was insti-
tuted in 1852; the first commander having been
Thomas C. Edwards. A new lodge in masonry,
Ivy, No. 397, was instituted in 1856.[105] It was
largely composed of young men. An adjunct of
the Masonic order, called The Southern Tier Masonic
Relief Association, was organized in 1868. The
Masonic Temple, where all these bodies named have

378, F. and A. M., which was instituted in July, 1855. Dr.
Corbett Peebles was its first W. M., and the meetings of the
lodge were held at his house. There was a Masonic Lodge
established in this township in 1810, holding its meetings in
an upper room of Capt. George Gordon's tavern. Daniel
E. Brown was its W. M. But the fact has almost faded
away from memory, as it has in fact. Other organizations
in this township are as follows: The Big Flats Ancient Order
of United Workmen, organized in March, 1879; an Equitable Aid Union, instituted on December 16, 1884, and the
Seeley Post No. 554, G. A. R., chartered April 25, 1885.
VAN ETTENVILLE has a Mount Lebanon Lodge, F. and
A M., chartered on July 12, 1877; the Van Ettenville
Lodge, Knights of Honor, organized April 19, 1879; a lodge
of the Knights and Ladies of Honor, instituted in 1883; an
Equitable Aid Union, organized in 1880; a "Provident
Shield Society," which began business on July 9, 1880, and
the Maxwell Post, G. A. R., organized in March, 1884.
BALDWIN has at North Chemung the North Chemung Grange,
Patrons of Husbandry, No. 277. VETERAN has, at Pine Val-
ley, Fidelity Lodge No. 157, I. O. G. T., organized on Febru-
ary 5, 1869, and Pine Valley Lodge No. 157, Order of Good
Templars, chartered in January, 1891, and at MILLPORT
The Old Oak Lodge No. 257, F. and A. M., organized on June
7, 1852.

[105]It held its first meeting on November 22, 1856. Its
first master was Thomas C. Edwards.

their meetings, was completed and occupied January 1, 1880. The post-office occupied this building twenty-three years.

Another order, the I. O. O. F., occupies no inconsiderable position in the annals of the county. Chemung Lodge, of this body, No. 127, was chartered on October 11, 1844.[106] The Fort Hill Encampment of this order, No. 18, was organized on February 13, 1846. Southern Tier Lodge, No. 344, was instituted on January 21, 1873. John T. Davidson was the first noble grand of this lodge. A German lodge of Odd Fellows, Donau; No. 363, was organized on June 30, 1873. Its first noble grand was Jacob Snyder. Another encampment, Elmira No. 86, I. O. O. F.; was organized on September 24, 1875, and from both the encampments was formed the Queen City Uniformed Patriarchs; on August 1, 1879. In Horseheads and Millport there were lodges of this order, but they were discontinued. In Breesport there was a lodge, Breesport No. 219, organized on February 11, 1875. Its first noble grand was George S. Sadler.

Patriotic organizations.—Baldwin Post; No. 6, G. A. R.; was among the very first of the Grand Army Posts that were organized, as its numerical designation indicates. It was organized June 11, 1868, its first commander having been Col. Gabriel L. Smith.

There have been many other organizations formed in Elmira with many purposes and objects

---

[106]The first officers of this lodge were: R. B. Sharpstein, N. G.; E. J. Horne, V. G.; D. C. Mallory, secretary; George P. Tyler, treasurer.

in view. In the musical way there have been
many brass bands that enjoyed high reputations,
in their time. The mention of the names of "Wisner's," "La Franc's," "Updegraff's," "The Em-
mett," and "Hager" during this period brings up
pleasant recollections in the minds of many. The
Germans were the most successful in undertakings
of this kind. Their Sangerbund, organized in 1856;
has had a long career along the lines for which it
was formed. Ernst Schidlen was its first president,
and Charles Mosgau its first leader.

Until 1878, when the paid Fire Department was
established in Elmira with Miles Trout as the first
chief engineer, there had been five fire companies.
Besides those already named there was organized
in 1854, "Young America" Company, No. 4, and
in the same year "Eureka Company; No. 5." The
first steam fire-engine used by the old Volunteer
Department, was bought the same year that Elmira
became a city. In 1850 two brick engine-houses
were built. In 1867 the Market Street hose tower
was erected, and the new building in the same place
was occupied in 1891.[107]

The military affairs of the county were well cared
for after the war. It was included in a regimental
district; the chief officer in command being Col.

---

[107]The other portions of the county had little or no protection from fire other than that of a most primitive character,
excepting Horseheads and Van Ettenville. In the first named
town, the Horseheads Steam and Hose Co., No. 1, was organized on August 22, 1873, John W. Lovell being foreman.
Acme Hose Co., No. 2, was organized on November 14, 1877.
The department was incorporated in June, 1876. Pioneer
Hose Co. was organized in 1874. In Van Ettenville the
Canfield Hook and Ladder Company was formed in January
1889.

Stephen T. Arnot. In 1874 the 110th Battalion was organized with Luther Caldwell in command. In Elmira there were three companies; one in Wellsburg, and one in Horseheads. There was also a battery· of artillery organized. But the system lasted only until 1878. The Thirtieth separate company soon after was formed; and is still in existence. The Armory, on Church Street, was built in 1886. In 1884, the brigadier-general commanding in this part of the State was taken from the Thirtieth Separate Company in the person of Gen. Edmund O. Beers. During the Spanish War this company served as D Company in one of the regiments from the western part of the State.

The Elmira Reformatory, which marked a new era in the penal institutions of the State, if not of the world, was occupied in 1876. The idea, of which the institution is a materialization, originated with Z. R. Brockway.[108]

Four charitable organizations mark the public interest manifested for the weak, the aged, and the unfortunate. The "Southern Tier Orphans' Home" was organized in 1868; the "Home for the

---

[108]MR. BROCKWAY had made the subject a study for forty years, and has seen it developed and successful. The amount of good it has accomplished is incalculable in the reclamation of many youths and young men who seemed to be wayward, but were set in the right path by the system adopted in the institution. A very unique publication is issued from the institution called *The Summary*, all of the work for which is done by the inmates. Its first number was printed on Thanksgiving Day, 1883. Mr. Brockway was elected Mayor of the city of Elmira in 1906, as the head and front of what has become known all over the United States, and formed a model in many communities, as "the Elmira Compact," a movement entered into by the political parties of the city to purify local politics and keep them clean.

Aged" had its first meeting in May; 1874; three years afterward its building was begun, and on July 1, 1880, it was completed and ready for occupancy. The "Industrial School" had its inception in 1877, but it was not until seven years later, in 1884, when the new building for its use was ready to be occupied. The Arnot-Ogden Hospital, admirably situated and perfectly equipped, was delivered in trust to its Board of Managers in December, 1888.

Along these same lines for doing good, with the charitable element eliminated, is the "Elmira Academy of Medicine," which was founded on June 29, 1852. Although its name indicated its locality, the membership was not confined to the city of Elmira.[109] The first president of the society was Dr. Erastus L. Hart. Among the out-of-town members was Dr. William Woodward, of Big Flats, a highly-esteemed man and physician. One object of this society was the collection and preservation of vital statistics. By this means; Elmira possesses a store of valuable information that runs farther back in the history of the valley than is possessed by very few cities or counties in the country.

The "Academy of Sciences" was established in September, 1861, by a number of gentlemen who desired to "look into things" that were curious and valuable. Its first president was the Rev. T. K. Beecher. It possesses an astronomical

---

[109]The constituent members of this organization were: Drs. H. S. Chubbuck, T. H. Squire, Ira F. Hart, Erastus L. Hart, Jotham Purdy, Uriah Smith, N. R. Derby, William C. Wey, J. K. Stanchfield. All of these stood high in the community, and with one exception are not now living.

observatory; in which is placed a large telescope; and the inquiries made by the organization extend to about all subjects in which it is aided by suitable apparatus of all kinds.

Bridges over the Chemung.—The Lake Street bridge suffered from fire in 1850, and was rebuilt. In 1853 another bridge was built from Main Street across the river, but it had many mishaps, being badly damaged by the great flood of 1865. In 1872 arrangements were made for substituting iron or steel bridges for these two. The Main Street bridge was finished on September 15, 1873, and the Lake Street bridge on October 1, 1874. Another new Lake Street bridge was constructed in 1905. Two other bridges, one at Madison Avenue, and the other at Walnut Street, were erected within the last decade of last century.

New banking facilities.—An institution called "The Bank of Elmira" was established in 1853. Its first president was David H. Tuthill; and its first cashier, Anson C. Ely. Out of this grew "The Second National Bank of Elmira," which was organized on December 14, 1863. Its first officers were: Henry M. Partridge, president; Daniel R. Pratt, vice-president; William F. Corey, cashier.[110]

There was a "First National Bank of Elmira" organized in 1863. But its life was of short duration. It fell into difficulties and went under the control of the Chemung Canal Bank.

There was a Farmers' and Mechanics' Bank

---

[110]This bank was the one hundred and forty-ninth institu- of that nature organized under the national banking laws. It has been a United States depository almost since its establishment.

established in Elmira in 1876, by Lewis M. Smith and Henry L. Bacon; but it is no longer in existence. The same may be said of the Elmira National Bank that was established in September, 1889. A private banking institution, established by the F. W. Dinniny influence about 1880, meets the wants of business men in the western part of the city.

Horseheads also has a bank, established about twenty years ago under the influence of the Bennitt family, of which John Bennitt, a descendant of Comfort Bennitt, who came very early into the valley; is at the head.

The Chemung Canal Bank for some years was a National Bank, but it withdrew its charter and became a State institution again about 1869. Recently, in 1903, it was consolidated with and became a part of the "Chemung Canal Trust Company," the first president of which was Ray Tompkins.

Amusements.—Elmira was always well provided with places for the amusement and entertainment of its citizens; some of which have already been mentioned. The old Opera House was built and occupied in 1868. It was succeeded by the Lyceum, which with the "Auditorium" was burned on March 6, 1904. The two buildings have been replaced, the first one having been occupied in 1905 and the last in 1906.

It seems strange that circus tents have been stretched on almost every prominent lot and corner in the city, and it is in the memory of many still living that the tall poles and white canvas could be seen on squares where now stand some of the fairest blocks and even churches that are in the city.

Racing has always been a favorite sport in the county, and some of the finest bred horses in the country have had their origin therein. From the very first settlement there have been tracks in the county that were famous in their time all over the State. Some of these were straightaway, like the one in Southport, or the one in Elmira starting at the foot of Lake Street and stretching north without a curve toward the lake, most of them, however, were circular or oval. There were two or three in Horseheads whose location can still be pointed out. One in Elmira, just west of the location of the "Rebel Prison" camp, a mile track, was immortalized in horse annals in 1860, during the continuance of a horse fair in the valley, by the appearance there of the famous mare "Flora Temple," who made one of her fastest miles then. In 1874 the Elmira Driving Park Association was organized, receiving the countenance and support of the best people in the city.[111] In July, 1886, the Maple Avenue Athletic Association for similar purposes was formed.

A notable event for the valley occurred in 1855, when the first fair of the State Agricultural Society was held in Elmira.[112] It had two features which

---

[111]At the inaugural meeting in the fall of 1875 one of the horses entered was "American Girl," who had a very fast record. During the race she fell forward dead at the three-quarter post. There was a slight rain falling at the time and a very distinct rainbow was formed. From the grand stand hundreds saw that the eastern end of it seemed to be resting on the dying mare's head.

[112]The address on this occasion was delivered by Governor

were subsequently dropped by the society on occasions of this kind, a formal address and a ball! There have been since five other State fairs held in the county, the last one in 1883.

The County Agricultural Society, which gives annually county fairs, was formed as early as 1853, Charles Hulett, of Horseheads, being the first president. In 1871, in conjunction with the State Society, 400 acres of land lying halfway between Elmira and Horseheads were secured and laid out for holding the fairs.

Farmer's clubs.—In December, 1869, there was held a meeting of farmers in a wagon shop, at Carr's Corners, in the suburbs of Elmira, that was destined to exert a great influence on the agricultural interests of the whole country. It was the first time that practical farmers got together and discussed matters about the farm that they were familiar with in their everyday life and knew from their own eyes and hands what they were talking about. Then was organized the "Elmira Farmers' Club," the model of a great many others all over the country.[113] Its first president was George W.

Grimes, of Iowa, a stately Daniel Webster style of man of the old school of oratory. The ball was in Floral Hall, and was one of the social events of the countryside that had never before been equaled in the valley, and has never since been very much surpassed.

[113] GEORGE W. HOFFMAN was a son of the William Hoffman who came very early to the valley. He has served as Alderman from his ward in the Common Council of the city of Elmira, and has been president of the State Agricultural Society. W. A. Armstrong established in 1874 the agricultural newspaper that he called the *Husbandman*, which attained a very wide circulation. He was at one time the head of the State organization of the "Patrons of Husbandry."

Hoffman, and its first secretary, W. A. Armstrong. There were no changes in these officers for many years. In 1873 the club built its hall in the near neighborhood of the place where it had held its first meeting, and it formed a pleasant and conspicuous object in the landscape.

In June, 1889, an organization calling itself the "Interstate Fair Association," was formed[114] for the purpose of giving annual exhibitions similar to county fairs. Its grounds were the same as those belonging to the "Maple Avenue Athletic Association."

The baseball annals of the valley deserve recognition, for they are regarded with much interest. Some of the most conspicuous citizens of Elmira were adepts at the game in their school and college days. In 1880, a team backed by the *Telegram* newspaper, achieved great prominence and success, and during the season of 1906 the "Father Mathew" nine made a great record.

In 1872, largely through the efforts of Geo. M. Diven, Esq., a street railway company was formed, and tracks laid connecting the city of Elmira and the village of Horseheads. In 1886 the company was sold to interests represented by Col. D. C. Robinson, and the tracks were greatly extended.

Electric lighting was introduced into Elmira in 1883, the company becoming the "Elmira Illuminating Company."

An Elmira Water Company was formed on April

---

[114]The first officers of this organization were: Judson H. Clark, president; George M. Robinson, secretary; D. C. Robinson, treasurer; George Brand, general superintendent.

14, 1859, and ten years afterward, in 1869, it was
reorganized and called the Elmira Water Works
Company, at whose head was Gen. A. S. Diven.

All of these companies; with the gas company
added thereto, came under the control of a large
corporation, and more recently were all taken over
by the Elmira Light, Water, and Railroad Company. This corporation has recently very greatly
extended its business, and in 1906 formed connection with a trolley line connecting Elmira with
Watkins and the head of Seneca Lake.

On August 29, 1879, the centennial of the Battle of Newtown was celebrated by the dedication
of a monument to General Sullivan; near the spot
where the engagement was fought.[115] It was located
on a practically inaccessible spot; and could not have
the care it called for and was entitled to. It has
therefore largely fallen to pieces. An effort has
recently been begun to have a new and more suitable memorial raised in a more conspicuous location.

Public journals.—The newspaper field in the
county was well occupied during this period. In
1869, a weekly journal, called the *Saturday Review*,
was started, but it was too fine and delicate to live.
It touched subjects that did not appeal to the
mass of the citizens. In 1879 there was a little

---

[115]This celebration was attended by the largest concourse
of people ever gathered together in the county. It was
estimated that between 25,000 and 30,000 persons were
present. Among the distinguished men who delivered
speeches were Gen. W. T. Sherman; Governor Henry P.
Hoyt, of Pennsylvania, and his staff; Governor Nat. Head
of New Hampshire and staff, and Governor Lucius Robinson,
of New York, and staff.

daily, with the striking and attractive name of the *Midday Sun;* run for a while in the interest of the Greenback political organization. If it carried out its name it should have been very bright. It was. Too bright to exist long. It turned itself out. It was followed the next year by the *Bazoo,* controlled by Hugh Coyle, and in the interest of the same political organization. Its name was changed to the *Evening Herald,* and then it passed into the "pi" box. In 1873 the *Weekly Free Press* was started in Horseheads, which was removed in 1878 to Elmira; and a daily issued in 1880. In 1884 it was consolidated with the *Gazette.* In 1874 the *Southern Tier Leader* was issued weekly for three years; and then stopped. The Chemung County *Republican* was published in Horseheads in 1856; being discontinued in 1858, and consolidated with the Elmira *Advertiser.* The Horseheads *Philosopher* was started for political reasons in 1856; by Samuel C. Taber.[116] It didn't last long although it won. The Horseheads *Journal* was first printed on April 16, 1858. In 1878 it was removed to Elmira; and espousing the Greenback theories changed its name to the Chemung County *Greenbacker.* It was removed back to Horseheads on April 14, 1887, and is now called the Chemung Valley *Reporter;* is published by a company under the editorship of George L. Mulford, a clean, bright;

[116]MR. TABER came to the valley in 1847 from Herkimer County, N. Y., and was engaged on several newspapers, especially on the Elmira *Advertiser,* where he won what might easily be called fame as a wit and genial companion with all. No man in the county enjoys the friendship, almost affection, of so many prominent men of the day.

well printed local sheet. There was a little newspaper published in 1874 called the Elmira *Enterprise*. It was a very creditable sheet being in the
hands of a young woman. But she married, and
the newspaper was no more. During the "Know-
Nothing" excitement of 1856, there was a weekly
issued called the *American's Own*. It did not flour-
ish any more than the notions it advocated. There
was a newspaper printed in the German language,
called the Chemung County *Journal*. Its first number was issued in 1875, and it lasted just three
years. There have been several unsuccessful attempts to establish Sunday newspapers in Elmira.
The Sunday *Times*, begun in 1878, didn't last a
year. The Sunday *Tidings* ran several years. It
didn't stop, but emigrated to Buffalo, N. Y., and
the Sunday *Republican* came out three or four
times and then disappeared.

Some industries and interests have their newspapers advocating their own ideas. In 1850 there
was a monthly called the *Temperance Gem*, whose
name indicated its purpose. A monthly in the
interest of the Conductors' Brotherhood was published for some years in Elmira, while its editor,
Calvin S. Wheaton, was a resident there. The
First Methodist Church has its *Quarterly Register*,
and Trinity Church its *Record*. The Young Men's
Christian Association publish a *Young Men's Journal*, and the college for women its quarterly, *The
Sibyl*.

A monthly general magazine named *The Argosy*
was published for a while in Elmira.

The *News*, an evening penny paper, was started

in 1894. The *Morning Sun* was published four
times only, in January, 1895.

The *Gazette* is the oldest newspaper in the county.
In 1856, then edited by William C. Rhodes, it
issued a daily edition for one year. Its management has seen many changes. In September,
1870, it was made into a stock company, the president of which was the Hon. David B. Hill. On
April 30, 1860, its daily edition was resumed.

The *Advertiser* was started on November 3, 1853,
being called Fairman's *Daily Advertiser*, and dis-
tributed free as an advertising sheet. It was
issued from the job printing office of the brothers
Seymour B. and Charles G. Fairman.[111] The newspaper became a daily on February 19, 1855. It,
too, has had numerous changes in its management.
In October, 1870, it became a corporation or an
association. In April, 1882, Mr. Fairman left the
company, and it came under the control of another
organization, of which the Hon. J. Sloat Fassett
was the head.

On May 7, 1879, the first number of the Elmira
Telegram was issued by three young men, Charles
Hazard, Henry S. Brooks, and James Hill. It has
had a remarkable career of prominence and prosperity.

---

[111]CHARLES G. FAIRMAN became one of the best-known men
and newspaper man in the State. He possessed unusual
faculties of facility and felicity in the use of language in his
editorial writings. He represented his ward as Alderman in
the Common Council of the city of Elmira, coming to the
valley from Niagara County, N. Y., in 1845. He became
Grand Master of the Odd Fellows of the State of New York,
was postmaster of the city of Elmira eight years, and was
Superintendent of the State Insurance Department one term.

On May 24; 1888, the first number of the *Evening Star* was issued by Isaac Seymour Copeland⁣¹¹¹ and James S. Woodford. It is now almost in the twentieth year of its regular evening illumination.

High officials and eminent men.—The county has the honor and credit of supplying to the nation and State many distinguished men; more it would seem than could have been expected from the small area it occupies on the map. Some of these, not already accounted for elsewhere in this little book, are: The Right Rev. DANIEL S. TUTTLE; Bishop of Missouri, and the presiding bishop of the Episcopal Church of the United States. He belongs to the family of the same name that very early came into the town of Big Flats, and had very much to do with its history. The Hon. LUCIUS ROBINSON. He was a descendant of Dr. John Robinson; one who came over in the famous *Mayflower*. He came to Elmira in 1855, and was prominent in business and political matters for his whole life. He was member of Assembly; Comptroller of the State twice, a member of the Constitutional Convention of 1871, and Governor of the State. The Hon. DAVID B. HILL. He was born in Chemung County; and came to Elmira in 1864; served the city as Alderman and Mayor; was elected Lieutenant-Governor in 1883; and Governor for three terms. In 1891 he was chosen to represent

---

¹¹¹MR. COPELAND is a nephew of Seymour Fairman and his brother, Charles G. Fairman, being named for the former. There seems to have been much of what might be called first-class newspaper blood in the Fairman family. It was well developed in the brothers and seems somehow to have got into the veins of the nephew.

the State of New York in the U. S. Senate.   Rear-Admiral FRANCIS A. ROE, U. S. N.   He was the son of Isaac Roe, a very prominent man in the early history of the valley, and especially in the annals of the Methodist Church.   He served with great credit in the Civil War.   He died at Washington, D. C., on December 28, 1901.   Rear-Admiral AARON KONKLE HUGHES.   He was born in Elmira and is descended on both sides of his house from settlers that early came to the valley.   He also served gallantly in the Civil War. He died in Washington, D. C., in 1905. Rear-Admiral THOMAS PERRY, U. S. N.   He also was born in Elmira, and also descended on both sides from the earliest settlers of the valley.   Lieutenant-Commander LEWIS S. VAN DUZER, U. S. N. He was born in Horseheads and is on the high road to positions of importance in the arm of the service to which he is attached.   FRANCIS COLLINGWOOD, also born in Elmira, and educated in its public schools.   He is one of the most eminent engineers of the country; has been connected with very important undertakings, and was very prominent in the construction of the first East River bridge in New York.   The Hon. JOHN ARNOT, JR., who enjoyed the unique experience of making his second canvas for member of Congress in a populous district without any one to contest the matter with him.   He had been repeatedly Mayor of the city of Elmira.   The Hon. J. SLOAT FASSETT.   He was born in Elmira, being descended from one who, during revolutionary times, was of immense assistance financially to the new and struggling gov-

ernment, and was poorly recompensed therefor.
Mr. Fassett has been District-Attorney of the county,
a member of the State Senate, Secretary of the
Republican National Committee, member of Congress; and has a future full of promise of still higher
honors. The Hon. SEYMOUR DEXTER. He came
to Elmira in 1864, was County Judge for two terms,
member of Assembly, and president of the Second
National Bank of Elmira. He was greatly interested in the matter of Building and Loan Associations, having made a thorough study of it, and published a book on the subject; which had a large
sale and is still an authority thereof. He died on
May 5, 1904. The Hon. H. BOARDMAN SMITH.
He came to Elmira in 1850, and was during his
lifetime a notable man in the professional, political, social, and Christian life of his time. He had
few equals as a public speaker. He served two
terms as member of Congress, and was Justice of
the Supreme Court of the State. He died in 1888.
The Hon. JOHN B. STANCHFIELD. He was born in
Elmira; a son of Dr. J. K. Stanchfield, a wise and
skilful physician. Mr. Stanchfield has been Mayor
of the city of Elmira, and member of Assembly.
Gen. EDWARD M. HOFFMAN. He was also a descendant of one of the earliest settlers of the valley,
whose name is frequently on the records and annals
of the county. He was very prominent in military
affairs from his youth. He became the Adjutant-
General of the State, and died suddenly while in the
discharge of his duties, on May 19, 1901, having
developed an unusual aptitude and skill in the
management of the military affairs of the State.

Col. ARCHIE BAXTER. He came to Elmira in 1880 from Steuben County; N. Y. His record in the Civil War was one of which any officer could justly be proud. He was County Clerk of Chemung County for one term; and became U. S. Marshal for the Northern District of New York. Few public speakers equal him on the platform; and he is constantly in demand for all sorts of occasions. He has the unusual distinction of having served as clerk of the New York State Assembly for fourteen years. EDWARD B. YOUMANS, ESQ. He came to Elmira in 1870, served on the Elmira Board of Education for several years, was chairman of the Democratic County Committee through several campaigns, and was the Chief Clerk of the Treasury Department in Washington for four years. He died in 1892. It may not be exactly accurate to claim that Samuel L. Clemens (Mark Twain), was supplied to the world and mankind by the county; but it is certain that he lived there several years; wrote many of his works in his little cottage on "Quarry Farm," on the hills east of Elmira, and chose for his wife a member of a family the head of which came very early into the valley. We can correctly say that "once tarried he here."

AT THE END.—It would seem eminently proper that at the conclusion of a little book like this some further account of the sacred spots where are laid away forever the bodies of those who have passed away should be given. What was called the Second Street Cemetery[119] in Elmira; laid out

[119]The first burial in this spot was that of the body of Mrs. Dr. E. L. Hart, the services being performed in the summer of 1839.

in 1838, then far in the country, now almost in the
center of the city, was in use for twenty years, when
a new association was formed, the plot chosen
dedicated by public services on October 9, 1858,
and called "Woodlawn." The first body buried
there, and at this time, was that of Col. John Hendy,
which was taken from the Main Street burying-
ground and deposited in a permanent spot, from
where it had laid since 1840. In 1877, all the bodies
buried in the Main Street ground were also removed
and placed in a separate spot in "Woodlawn,"
leaving the ground to be a part of Main Street
Park.[120] There are cemeteries in Elmira in which
the bodies are buried of those belonging to the
Roman Catholic and Hebrew faiths. They lie
near each other and were both dedicated about
1850.

---

[120]In Horseheads and Breesport there are well-kept cemeteries. In the Breesport one, the first person buried was
one by the name of Schoonover. In Horseheads the first
purchase of land for the purpose was made in 1856. By subsequent purchases the ground became eleven acres in extent.
It is under the management of the village board. In Van
Etten village the cemetery is called "Mount Hope." It
lies within the boundaries of the corporation and the plot
was purchased on December 1, 1879. In Erin there is an
association called the "Scotchtown Cemetery Association,"
which was organized on February 11, 1881. In Veteran
at Pine Valley, the Pine Valley Cemetery Association was
incorporated on May 5, 1883. Previous to this the burying
ground was on a knoll near the Baptist Church. The cemetery near the village is now used. In Millport the first burial
ground was on the old Bently farm, and there many of the
bodies of the old settlers lie. The Millport Cemetery Association was incorporated on November 18, 1870. It has
control of the cemetery east of the village. The Big Flats
Cemetery Association was incorporated on July 24, 1855,
William A. Tuttle being the president of the organization.
By various purchases the extent of the plot amounts to
about four acres.

PART V

Recapitulation of Important Events
Happening in the County

Recapitulation of Important Events
HAPPENING IN THE COUNTY.

1779—August 29—Battle of Newtown and the beginning of
the History of Chemung County.

1786—Isaac Baldwin and eight sons settle in Chemung.

1787—Timothy Smith settles in Southport.

—John Breese settles in Horseheads.

—Christian Mynheer (Minier) settles in Big Flats.

1788—Abraham Miller settles in Southport.

—Abner M. Hetfield settles in Southport.

—John Hendy settles in Elmira.

—Township of Chemung erected, being a part of Montgomery County.

—Green Bentley settles in Wellsburg.

1789—Eunice Kelsey, first white child born in Wellsburg.

1790—Village of Newtown laid out.

1791—Final treaty with the Indians at Elmira.

1792—April 10—Township of Newtown erected from Chemung Township.

—First sawmill built in Wellsburg by Abner and Henry
Wells.

1793—June 28—First Masonic lodge, Union No. 30, organized
in the county.

1795—Joel Thomas settles in Van Etten.

—Gen. Jacob Swartwood settles at Swartwood.

—First Presbyterian minister the Rev. Daniel Thatcher,
comes to Elmira.

1796—First Court House erected at Newtown.

1797—The valley visited by the Duke of Orleans, who became the King of the French.

1798—First settler in Veteran, Green Bentley.

—Van Ettenville first settled.

—First school-house, a log one, built in Newtown.

1801—January 1—First post-office established in the county
at Newtown, Aaron Konkle, postmaster.

—April 1—First post-office established in town of Chemung, George W. Buck, postmaster.

1807—July 1—First turnpike through the county from
Elmira to Seneca Lake.

1808—April 6—Township of Elmira formed from Chemung.

1812—Newtown regularly included in Methodist circuit.

—First Baptist Church built in Wellsburg.

—First settlers in town of Baldwin, Charles and War-
ren Granger.

1815—First settler in Erin, Basil Sperry.

—First newspaper printed in county, the *Investigator*.

—March—Village of Newtown incorporated.

1816—First settler in Catlin, Capt. John Martin

1818—Stephen Tuttle settles in Newtown.

—First frame building erected in Van Ettenville by
James Van Etten.

1819—First stage route established from Newtown to Wilkesbarre, Pa.

1820—First woolen mill set up in Southport by Silas Billings.

1822—March 29—Township of Erin formed.

—April 16—Township of Southport formed.

1823—April 16—Townships of Big Flats, Southport, Veteran,
and Catlin erected.

1823—Myron Collins establishes woolen mill in Veteran.

1824—Court House built in Newtown; second one.

—First bridge built over the Chemung at Newtown.

—March 20—Township of Cayuta formed.

1826—January 29—First dam over the Chemung River
built.

—First brick house built in Elmira by Matthew Mc-
Reynolds.

1827—First restaurant opened in Elmira.

1828—First tavern built in Horseheads by James Shute.

—April 21—Name of village of Newtown changed to
Elmira, and the village incorporated.

1829—First brick building erected in Chemung by Isaac
Parshall.

1832—First store built in Southport by Isaac Reynolds.
—Chemung Canal completed.

1833—Famous brick hotel built in Southport: "Auster Portus Diversorun."
—January 2—First post-office established in Erin, William D. Stewart, postmaster.
—April 9—Chemung Canal Bank chartered.

1834—The "Elmira Guards" organized; first military company in the county.
—January—The "Elmira Mechanic's Society" organized.
—March 31—Trinity Church in Elmira organized.
—May—First fire-engine for Elmira bought.

1836—March 29—Chemung County organized.
—May 8—Chemung County Medical Society organized.

1837—May—Horseheads incorporated as a village under the name of Fairport.

1840—June 25—Post-office established in Lowmanville under the name of West Chemung.

1846—First telegraph in the county.
—January 4—Park Church in Elmira organized

1847—Photography introduced in Elmira.

1848—First hotel built in Pine City.

1849—Illuminating gas introduced in Elmira.
—Burning of the Eagle Tavern.
—December—The New York and Erie Railroad finished to Elmira.

1853—First store built in Lowmanville by George Lowman.
—Elmira College for Women opened.

1854—February 8—Township of Horseheads erected.
—April 17—Township of Van Etten erected.
—April 17—Portions of Chemung County taken to help make the new county of Schuyler.
—June 22—Post-office established in Catlin, Joseph Cooper, postmaster.

1854—August 1—Elmira and Williamsport Railroad opened.

1856—April 7—Township of Baldwin erected.

1858—July 1—First meeting of the Elmira Young Men's Christian Association.

1859—Elmira Board of Education organized.

CHEMUNG COUNTY, N. Y.

1896—New City Hall in Elmira built.

—Village of Elmira Heights incorporated.

1899—New charter for the City of Elmira providing for twelve wards.

1900—March 14—Death of the Rev. T. K. Beecher.

1903—September 13—New Federal building in Elmira occupied.

—October 14—Monument to the Volunteer Fire Department unveiled at Woodlawn.

1904—March 6—The Lyceum and Auditorium buildings burned.

1905—April 10—The Elmira Chamber of Commerce organized.

1905—The Lyceum and Auditorium reopened.

—The Lake Street bridge completed.

www.ingramcontent.com/pod-product-compliance
Lightning Source LLC
Chambersburg PA
CBHW051813040426
42446CB00007B/650